WITHDRAWN

JUL 0 3 2024

DAVID O. McKAY LIBRARY
BYU-IDAHO

STORY-TELLING BALLADS

STORY-TELLING BALLADS

SELECTED AND ARRANGED FOR
STORY-TELLING AND READING ALOUD
AND FOR
THE BOYS' AND GIRLS' OWN READING

BY

FRANCES JENKINS OLCOTT

GRANGER POETRY LIBRARY

GRANGER BOOK CO., INC.
Great Neck, N.Y.

FIRST PUBLISHED   1920

REPRINTED   1982

LC 81-84881
ISBN 0-89609-234-8

Printed in the U.S.A.

TO MY SISTER
VIRGINIA OLCOTT

THE FOREWORD

HERE are 77 story-telling ballads and narrative poems, that will make the heart beat faster and the pulse bound, of any boy or girl from twelve to fifteen years of age.

They offer a feast of good things — romances, hero-tales, Faërie legends, and adventures of Knights and lovely Damsels. They sing of proud and wicked folk, of gentle and loyal ones, of Laidley Worms, Witches, Mermaids with golden combs, sad maidens, glad ones and fearless lovers, moss-troopers, border-rievers, and Kings in disguise. All their doings are related in the stirring, leaping, joyous — or at times martial and mournful-ballad measure.

The ancient ballads are here presented exactly as when in days of old they were sung by minstrels and recited by gaffers and gammers. No alterations are made in the texts of the ballad-collectors and collators, except the changing of a few objectionable words. Two or three of the less well-known ballads are done into modern spelling. A number, not hitherto found in children's collections, will be delightfully new to young people. Some popular ballads, like "King John and the Abbot of Canterbury," and "The King and the

Miller of Mansfield," are omitted because they are in *Story-Telling Poems*.

A goodly number of famous modern ballads are included; and at the end of the volume are 10 short narrative poems of "Pilgrimage and Souls so Strong."

At the end of the book are a Glossary and Indexes of subjects, authors, titles, and first lines.

TEACHERS, STORY-TELLERS, AND BALLADS

SINCE great care has been taken to choose authoritative texts (see Acknowledgments, page xv and Suggestions for Teachers, page 363), the teacher will find this collection helpful when instructing classes in early English literature or in ballad structure and measure.

The Glossary for classroom use is placed at the back of the book, not in footnotes, because children who are reading for enjoyment easily learn new words from the context.

The collection may be used for story-hours; or, as older boys and girls prefer being read aloud to, in it may be found an abundance of material for weekly poetry hours and for memorizing.

YOUTH IN THE BALLADS

BALLADS are the natural heritage of every boy and girl. Ballads are tuned to the very pulse of Youth. They are red-blooded: joyous with the freshness of Springtime, and robust with the early Summer of Life. They appeal with peculiar delight to growing boys and girls, satisfying, as do no other poems, their craving for emotional expression in quick, rhythmic form.

Ballads not only feed the romantic spirit of young people, but teach them much homely wisdom. They are essentially democratic and human. In them Kings and tinkers, Knights and shepherds, meet, talk, and feast together like comrades.

And because the vigour of Youth so animates the old ballads, young folk read them eagerly, learn them almost without effort, and recite them with gusto. The wild, free life in the good greenwood, the chivalry, mystery, pathos, heroic deeds, and thrilling experiences — in fact, Life itself running the whole gamut of human emotions — enthrall the ever eager, questioning, shifting moods of boys and girls.

HOW THE BALLADS GREW

THE human and universal in the ancient ballads, their eternal youthful appeal, are rooted deepset in the daily life of the People. Their very meter and airs are natural growths like the sheath of a wildflower. For in those good old ballad-making days, minstrels, the welcome guests of rich and poor, wandered from castle to cot and inn,

from eyrie-like retreats of Highland chiefs to
fortified border-towers of the Lowland or "North
Contraye." And as the minstrels rested their
harps or bagpipes on the earthen floors of cot-
tages, or while they sat feasting with nobles in
baronial halls, they heard peasants, working-folk,
servitors, squires, ladies, and returned Crusaders, telling of their adventures on land and sea,
in fights, battles, border-raids, in abductions of
lovely maidens, in combats with Saracens and
with Laidley monsters, in meetings with Faërie
Knights and Elfin Queens all under the green-
wood-shade. They heard, also, tales of change-
lings and visits to Fairyland; stories of Ghosts,
Ghouls, and Witches; legends of the sea; and
traditions of national heroes.

This material, so varied, so freshly spontaneous
and imaginative, the minstrels shaped into ballads, setting them to music now wild and weird,
now tragic and mournful, now sweet and debonair.
So they played and sang the ballads in cottage,
bower, and hall, moulding them to the delight
and humours of their hearers, changing them to
suit time and place. Thus there grew up many
versions of a single ballad.

The old folk, too, the gaffers and gammers by
the fireside, learned the ballads and recited or
sung them to the children; who in their turn,
when they became old, told them to other chil-

dren. Thus the old songs were passed along by word of mouth from generation to generation, from countryside to countryside, and even from one land to another.

MAKING A COLLECTION FOR CHILDREN

As was natural in those coarse old times, much that was unsuitable for children was woven into the ballads; which to-day makes it a difficult task to compile a representative juvenile collection. For, as Spenser so aptly put it when writing of Irish bards, they "seldom use to choose unto themselves the doings of good men for the arguments of their poems, but whomsoever they find to be . . . most bold and lawless in his doings, most dangerous and desperate in all parts of disobedience and rebellious disposition, him they set up and glorify in their rhymes, him they praise to the people, and to young men make an example to follow."

But Spenser's criticism of the Irish bards is far too violent a stricture on all Scottish and English ballad literature. For there are Scottish and English ones, clean, merry, and nobly heroic; fine and wholesome reading for our boys and girls.

For Sir Walter Scott's romantic tastes and his interest in Highland and Border life were awakened and fired, when he was a boy, by reading ballads. And Sir Philip Sydney wrote in his *De-fence of Poetry*, "Certainly, I must confess mine own barbarousness; I never heard the old song of Percy and Douglas, that I found not my heart moved more than with a trumpet; and yet it is sung but by some blind crowder, with no rougher voice than rude style . . . In Hungary I have seen it the manner at all feasts, and all other such-like meetings, to have songs of their ancestors' valour, which that right soldier-like nation think one of the chiefest kindlers of brave courage."

But in making a collection of ballads for modern boys and girls, it is not enough to choose those that will arouse only the higher emotions. The interests of young people have to be consulted; while nothing in extremely difficult Scottish dialect may be included, nor in very old English.

Then there are many versions of individual ballads to choose from. Of "Hynd Horn" there are eight or more; of "Young Beichan and Susie Pye," fourteen or more; and of other ballads many versions. Next, authoritative texts must be found, for some transcribers have made mistakes or have altered the originals. So it may be seen what a painstaking task it is to compile a collection of ballads for educational purposes as well as for the boys' and girls' own reading.

As for this volume, it covers so wide a range

of fascinating subjects that it will surely entrance any lad or lass who, opening its pages for pleasure-reading, steps with Valentine and Ursine, Robin Hood and Clorinda, and the brave outlaw Murray, into

The gude green-wood amang the lily flower.

ACKNOWLEDGMENTS

My thanks are due Messrs. Houghton Mifflin Company for the use of the following modern ballads, "The Ballad of the Oysterman," by Oliver Wendell Holmes; "The Luck of Edenhall," "The Three Kings," and "The Skeleton in Armour," by Henry Wadsworth Longfellow; "The Singing Leaves," by James Russell Lowell; "Barclay of Ury," by John Greenleaf Whittier.

Among the authoritative texts from which I have taken ancient and popular ballads, are Bell's *Early Ballads and Songs of the Peasantry of England;* Bishop Percy's *Reliques of Ancient English Poetry*, and his *Folio Manuscript, edited by Hales and Furnivall; A Collection of Old Ballads*, London, 1723–25; Dixon's *Ancient Poems, Ballads, and Songs of the Peasantry of England* (Percy Society); Jamieson's *Popular Ballads and Songs;* Monk Lewis's *Tales of Wonder;* Motherwell's *Minstrelsy, Ancient and Modern;* Nicholson's *Historical and Traditional Tales . . . Connected with the South of Scotland;* Ritson's *Robin Hood;* Sir Walter Scott's *Minstrelsy of the Scottish Border;* Sheldon's *Minstrelsy of the English Border;* also the scholarly collection of *English and Scottish Popular Ballads*, compiled and edited by Professor Francis

James Child, for the use of which my acknowledgments are due its publishers, Messrs. Houghton Mifflin Company.

The best texts available have been followed for the original ballads by Sir Walter Raleigh, George Herbert, Hogg, Scott, Lover, Kingsley, Tennyson, Campbell, and Keats.

CONTENTS

xviii   CONTENTS

CONTENTS

CONTENTS

THE SALT BLUE SEAS

THE STORMY WINDS DO BLOW

One Friday morn when we set sail,
   Not very far from land,
We there did espy a fair pretty maid
   With a comb and a glass in her hand, her hand, her hand,
   With a comb and a glass in her hand.

    While the raging seas did roar,
      And the stormy winds did blow,
    While we jolly sailor-boys were up into the top,
      And the land-lubbers lying down below, below, below,
      And the land-lubbers lying down below.

Then up starts the captain of our gallant ship,
   And a brave young man was he:
"I've a wife and a child in fair Bristol town,
   But a widow I fear she will be."

Then up starts the mate of our gallant ship,
   And a bold young man was he:
"Oh! I have a wife in fair Portsmouth town,
   But a widow I fear she will be."

Then up starts the cook of our gallant ship,
   And a gruff old soul was he:
"Oh! I have a wife in fair Plymouth town,
   But a widow I fear she will be."

And then up spoke the little cabin-boy,
   And a pretty little boy was he:
"Oh! I am more grievd for my daddy and my mammy
   Than you for your wives all three."

Then three times round went our gallant ship,
   And three times round went she:
For the want of a life-boat they all went down,
   And she sank to the bottom of the sea.

    While the raging seas did roar,
      And the stormy winds did blow,
    While we jolly sailor-boys were up into the top,
      And the land-lubbers lying down below, below, below,
      And the land-lubbers lying down below.

SIR PATRICK SPENS

THE king sits in Dunfermline town,
　　Drinking the blude-red wine;
"O whare will I get a skeely skipper,
　　To sail this new ship of mine?"

O up and spake an eldern knight,
　　Sat at the king's right knee, —
"Sir Patrick Spens is the best sailor,
　　That ever sailed the sea." —

Our king has written a braid letter,
　　And seal'd it with his hand,
And sent it to sir Patrick Spens,
　　Was walking on the strand.

"To Noroway, to Noroway,
　　To Noroway o'er the faem;
The king's daughter of Noroway,
　　'T is thou maun bring her hame."

The first word that sir Patrick read,
　　Sae loud loud laughed he;
The neist word that sir Patrick read,
　　The tear blinded his ee.

"O wha is this has done this deed,
  And tauld the king o' me,
To send us out, at this time of the year,
  To sail upon the sea?

"Be it wind, be it weet, be it hail, be it sleet,
  Our ship must sail the faem;
The king's daughter of Noroway,
  'T is we must fetch her hame." —

They hoysed their sails on Monenday morn,
  Wi' a' the speed they may;
They hae landed in Noroway,
  Upon a Wodensday.

They hadna been a week, a week,
  In Noroway, but twae,
When that the lords o' Noroway
  Began aloud to say, —

"Ye Scottishmen spend a' our king's goud,
  And a' our queenis fee." —
"Ye lie, ye lie, ye liars loud!
  Fu' loud I hear ye lie:

"For I brought as much white monie,
  As gane my men and me,
And I brought a half-fou o' gude red goud,
  Out o'er the sea wi' me.

"Make ready, make ready, my merrymen a'!
  Our gude ship sails the morn," —
"Now, ever alake, my master dear,
  I fear a deadly storm!

"I saw the new moon, late yestreen,
  Wi' the auld moon in her arm;
And, if we gang to sea, master,
  I fear we 'll come to harm."

They hadna sail'd a league, a league,
  A league but barely three,
When the lift grew dark, and the wind blew loud,
  And gurly grew the sea.

The ankers brak, and the top-masts lap,
  It was sic a deadly storm;
And the waves cam o'er the broken ship,
  Till a' her sides were torn.

"O where will I get a gude sailor,
  To take my helm in hand,
Till I get up to the tall top-mast;
  To see if I can spy land?" —

"O here am I, a sailor gude,
  To take the helm in hand,
Till you go up to the tall top-mast;
  But I fear you 'll ne'er spy land."

He hadna gane a step, a step,
  A step but barely ane,
When a bout flew out of our goodly ship,
  And the salt sea it cam in.

"Gae, fetch a web o' the silken claith,
  Another o' the twine,
And wap them into our ship's side,
  And letna the sea come in." —

They fetch'd a web o' the silken claith,
  Another o' the twine,
And they wapp'd them round that gude ship's side,
  But still the sea cam in.

O laith, laith, were our gude Scots lords
  To weet their cork-heel'd shoon!
But lang or a' the play was play'd,
  They wat their hats aboon.

And mony was the feather bed,
  That flatter'd on the faem;
And mony was the gude lord's son,
  That never mair cam hame.

The ladyes wrang their fingers white,
  The maidens tore their hair,
A' for the sake of their true loves;
  For them they 'll see na mair.

O lang, lang, may the ladyes sit,
  Wi' their fans into their hand,
Before they see sir Patrick Spens
  Come sailing to the strand!

And lang, lang, may the maidens sit,
  With their goud kaims in their hair,
A'waiting for their ain dear loves!
  For them they'll see nae mair.

O forty miles off Aberdeen,
  'T is fifty fathoms deep,
And there lies gude sir Patrick Spens,
  Wi' the Scots lords at his feet.

THE DÆMON LOVER

"O WHERE have you been, my long, long love,
  This long seven years and mair?"
"O I'm come to seek my former vows
  Ye granted me before."

"O hold your tongue of your former vows,
  For they will breed sad strife;
O hold your tongue of your former vows,
  For I am become a wife."

He turned him right and round about,
  And the tear blinded his ee:
"I wad never hae trodden on Irish ground,
  If it had not been for thee.

"I might hae had a king's daughter,
   Far, far beyond the sea;
I might have had a king's daughter,
   Had it not been for love o thee."

"If ye might have had a king's daughter,
   Yer sel ye had to blame;
Ye might have taken the king's daughter,
   For ye kend that I was nane.

"If I was to leave my husband dear,
   And my two babes also,
O what have you to take me to,
   If with you I should go?"

"I hae seven ships upon the sea —
   The eighth brought me to land —
With four-and-twenty bold mariners,
   And music on every hand."

She has taken up her two little babes,
   Kissd them baith cheek and chin:
"O fair ye weel, my ain two babes,
   For I'll never see you again."

She set her foot upon the ship,
   No mariners could she behold;
But the sails were o the taffetie,
   And the masts o the beaten gold.

She had not sailed a league, a league,
  A league but barely three,
When dismal grew his countenance,
  And drumlie grew his ee.

They had not saild a league, a league,
  A league but barely three,
Until she espied his cloven foot,
  And she wept right bitterlie.

"O hold your tongue of your weeping,"
    says he,
  "Of your weeping now let me be;
I will shew you how the lilies grow
  On the banks of Italy."

"O what hills are yon, yon pleasant hills,
  That the sun shines sweetly on?"
"O yon are the hills of heaven," he said,
  "Where you will never win."

"O whaten a mountain is yon," she said,
  "All so dreary wi frost and snow?"
"O yon is the mountain of hell," he cried,
  "Where you and I will go."

He strack the tap-mast wi his hand,
  The fore-mast wi his knee,
And he brake that gallant ship in twain,
  And sank her in the sea.

THE MERMAID

PART I

On Jura's heath how sweetly swell
    The murmurs of the mountain bee!
How softly mourns the writhed shell
    Of Jura's shore, its parent sea!

But softer, floating o'er the deep,
    The Mermaid's sweet sea-soothing lay,
That charmed the dancing waves to sleep,
    Before the bark of Colonsay.

Aloft the purple pennons wave,
    As parting gay from Crinan's shore,
From Morven's wars the seamen brave
    Their gallant Chieftain homeward bore.

In youth's gay bloom, the brave Macphail
    Still blamed the lingering bark's delay;
For her he chid the flagging sail,
    The lovely Maid of Colonsay.

"And raise," he cried, "the song of love,
    The maiden sung with tearful smile,
When first, o'er Jura's hills to rove,
    We left afar the lonely isle! —

"'When on this ring of ruby red .
   Shall die,' she said, 'the crimson hue,
Know that thy favourite fair is dead,
   Or proves to thee and love untrue.'"

Now, lightly poised, the rising oar
   Disperses wide the foamy spray,
And, echoing far o'er Crinan's shore,
   Resounds the song of Colonsay.

"Softly blow, thou western breeze,
   Softly rustle through the sail!
Soothe to rest the furrowy seas,
   Before my Love, sweet western gale!"

Thus, all to soothe the Chieftain's woe,
   Far from the maid he loved so dear,
The song arose, so soft and slow,
   He seemed her parting sigh to hear.

The lonely deck he paces o'er,
   Impatient for the rising day,
And still, from Crinan's moonlight shore,
   He turns his eyes to Colonsay.

The moonbeams crisp the curling surge,
   That streaks with foam the ocean green:
While forward still the rowers urge
   Their course, a female form was seen.

That Sea-maid's form, of pearly light,
  Was whiter than the downy spray,
And round her bosom, heaving bright,
  Her glossy, yellow ringlets play.

Borne on a foamy-crested wave,
  She reached amain the bounding prow,
Then clasping fast the Chieftain brave,
  She, plunging, sought the deep below.

Ah! long beside thy feigned bier,
  The monks the prayers of death shall say,
And long, for thee, the fruitless tear
  Shall weep the Maid of Colonsay!

PART II

BUT downwards, like a powerless corse,
  The eddying waves the Chieftain bear;
He only heard the moaning hoarse
  Of waters, murmuring in his ear.

The murmurs sink, by slow degrees;
  No more the surges round him rave;
Lulled by the music of the seas,
  He lies within a coral cave.

In dreamy mood reclines he long,
  Nor dares his tranced eyes unclose,
Till, warbling wild, the Sea-maid's song,
  Far in the crystal cavern, rose;

"This yellow sand, this sparry cave,
　　Shall bend thy soul to beauty's sway;
Canst thou the maiden of the wave
　　Compare to her of Colonsay?"

Roused by that voice, of silver sound,
　　From the paved floor he lightly sprung,
And, glancing wild his eyes around,
　　Where the fair Nymph her tresses wrung,

No form he saw of mortal mould;
　　It shone like ocean's snowy foam;
Her ringlets waved in living gold,
　　Her mirror crystal, pearl her comb.

Her pearly comb the Siren took,
　　And careless bound her tresses wild;
Still o'er the mirror stole her look,
　　As on the wondering youth she smiled.

Like music from the greenwood tree,
　　Again she raised the melting lay;
"Fair Warrior, wilt thou dwell with me,
　　And leave the Maid of Colonsay?

"Fair is the crystal hall for me,
　　With rubies and with emeralds set,
And sweet the music of the sea
　　Shall sing, when we for love are met.

"How sweet to dance, with gliding feet,
    Along the level tide so green,
Responsive to the cadence sweet,
    That breathes along the moonlight scene!

"And soft the music of the main
    Rings from the motley tortoise-shell,
While moonbeams, o'er the watery plain,
    Seem trembling in its fitful swell.

"Through the green meads beneath the sea,
    Enamoured, we shall fondly stray —
Then, gentle warrior, dwell with me,
    And leave the Maid of Colonsay!" —

"Though bright thy locks of glistening gold,
    Fair maiden of the foamy main!
Thy life-blood is the water cold,
    While mine beats high in every vein.

"Though all the splendour of the sea
    Around thy faultless beauty shine,
That heart, that riots wild and free,
    Can hold no sympathy with mine.

"These sparkling eyes, so wild and gay,
    They swim not in the light of love:
The beauteous Maid of Colonsay,
    Her eyes are milder than the dove!

"Even now, within the lonely isle,
  Her eyes are dim with tears for me;
And canst thou think that siren smile
  Can lure my soul to dwell with thee?"

An oozy film her limbs o'erspread;
  Unfolds in length her scaly train:
She tossed, in proud disdain, her head,
  And lashed, with webbed fin, the main.

"Dwell here, alone!" the Mermaid cried,
  "And view far off the Sea-nymphs play;
Thy prison-wall, the azure tide,
  Shall bar thy steps from Colonsay.

"Whene'er, like Ocean's scaly brood,
  I cleave, with rapid fin, the wave,
Far from the daughter of the flood,
  Conceal thee in this coral cave.

"I feel my former soul return;
  It kindles at thy cold disdain:
And has a mortal dared to spurn
  A daughter of the foamy main!" —

She fled; around the crystal cave
  The rolling waves resume their **road**
On the broad portal idly rave,
  But enter not the Nymph's abode.

And many a weary night went by,
  As in the lonely cave he lay;
And many a sun rolled through the sky,
  And poured its beams on Colonsay;

And oft, beneath the silver moon,
  He heard afar the Mermaid sing,
And oft, to many a melting tune,
  The shell-formed lyres of ocean ring:

And when the moon went down the sky,
  Still rose, in dreams, his native plain,
And oft he thought his love was by,
  And charmed him with some tender strain;

And heart-sick, oft he waked to weep,
  When ceased that voice of silver sound,
And thought to plunge him in the deep,
  That walled his crystal cavern round.

But still the ring, of ruby red,
  Retained its vivid crimson hue,
And each despairing accent fled,
  To find his gentle Love so true.

PART III

WHEN seven long lonely months were gone,
  The Mermaid to his cavern came,
No more misshapen from the zone,
  But like a maid of mortal frame.

"O give to me that ruby ring,
　That on thy finger glances gay,
And thou shalt hear the Mermaid sing
　The song, thou lovest, of Colonsay." —

"This ruby ring, of crimson grain,
　Shall on thy finger glitter gay,
If thou wilt bear me through the main,
　Again to visit Colonsay." —

"Except thou quit thy former Love,
　Content to dwell for aye with me,
Thy scorn my finny frame might move,
　To tear thy limbs amid the sea." —

"Then bear me swift along the main,
　The lonely isle again to see,
And, when I here return again,
　I plight my faith to dwell with thee." —

An oozy film her limbs o'erspread,
　While slow unfolds her scaly train.
With gluey fangs her hands were clad,
　She lashed, with webbed fin, the main.

He grasps the Mermaid's scaly sides,
　As, with broad fin, she oars her way;
Beneath the silent moon she glides,
　That sweetly sleeps on Colonsay.

Proud swells her heart! she deems, at last,
  To lure him with her silver tongue,
And, as the shelving rocks she past,
  She raised her voice, and sweetly sung.

In softer, sweeter strains she sung,
  Slow gliding o'er the moonlight bay,
When light to land the Chieftain sprung,
  To hail the Maid of Colonsay.

Oh! sad the Mermaid's gay notes fell,
  And sadly sink remote at sea!
So sadly mourns the writhed shell
  Of Jura's shore, its parent sea.

And ever as the year returns,
  The charm-bound sailors know the day,
For sadly still the Mermaid mourns
  The lovely Chief of Colonsay.

Dr. John Leyden. (*Condensed*)

A-HARROWING O' THE BORDER

THE GALLOWAY RAID

The reavers of Eskdale were mounted for weir,
And Annandale moss-troopers grasped the spear;
And the blades that they bore in the sun glittered bright;
And breast-plate and helmet reflected the light.

They spurred the fleet charger thro' bog and thro' brake;
To the yell of their slogan the echoes awake;
The Johnstones and Jardines cry, "Lads, we'll away,
And we'll foray the pastures of Fair Galloway!"

The men were determined — their steeds they were strong,
And eager for plunder they pranced along;
The clang of their weapons rung loud on the dale,
And their helmet-plumes waving aloft on the gale.

. . . .

Beholdst thou the beacon-light gleaming afar,
On misty Glenbennan, the signal of war?
Bengairn and Caerlochan their blazes display,
And they warn the bold spearmen of Fair Galloway.

But the damsels of Esk and of Annan may mourn,
And in vain may they look for their lovers' return;
On the green dale of Dryburgh they rest in their grave,
And o'er them the hemlock and rank nettles wave.

And few have escaped from the Galloway spear,
That followed the flying and glanced in their rear,
And the moss-troopers' widows are ruing the day
Their *husbands departed for Fair Galloway.*

(Condensed)

THE MORE MODERN BALLAD OF CHEVY-CHASE

PART I

God prosper long our noble King,
    Our liffes and saftyes all!
A woefull hunting once there was
    In Chevy-Chase befall.

To drive the deere with hound and horne,
    Erle Percy took the way;
The child may rue that is unborne
    The hunting of that day!

The stout Erle of Northumberland
    A vow to God did make,
His pleasure in the Scottish woods
    Three sommers days to take;

The cheefest harts in Chevy-Chase
    To kill and beare away.
These tydings to Erle Douglas came,
    In Scottland where he lay,

Who sent Erle Percy present word,
    He wold prevent his sport,
The English Erle, not fearing that,
    Did to the woods resort,

With fifteen hundred bowmen bold,
  All chosen men of might,
Who knew ffull well in time of neede
  To ayme their shafts arright.

The gallant greyhounds swiftly ran
  To chase the fallow deere;
On Munday they began to hunt
  Ere daylight did appeare;

And long before high noone they had
  A hundred fat buckes slaine.
Then having dined, the drovyers went
  To rouze the deare againe;

The bowmen mustered on the hills,
  Well able to endure;
Theire backsids all with speciall care,
  That day were guarded sure.

The hounds ran swiftly through the woods
  The nimble deere to take,
That with their cryes the hills and dales
  An eccho shrill did make.

Lord Percy to the quarry went
  To view the tender deere;
Quoth he, "Erle Douglas promised once
  This day to meete me heere;

'But if I thought he wold not come,
  Noe longer wold I stay."
With that, a brave younge gentlman
  Thus to the Erle did say,

"Loe, yonder doth Erle Douglas come,
  His men in armour bright,
Full twenty hundred Scottish speres
  All marching in our sight,

"All men of pleasant Tivydale,
  Fast by the river Tweede:"
"O ceaze your sportts!" Erle Percy said,
  "And take your bowes with speede.

"And now with me, my countrymen,
  Your courage forth advance!
For there was never champion yett
  In Scottland nor in France,

"That ever did on horsbacke come,
  But if my hap it were,
I durst encounter man for man,
  With him to breake a spere."

Erle Douglas on his milke white steede,
  Most like a Baron bold,
Rode formost of his company,
  Whose armour shone like gold.

"Shew me," sayd hee, "whose men you bee,
That hunt soe boldly heere,
That without my consent doe chase
And kill my fallow deere."

The first man that did answer make
Was noble Percy hee,
Who sayd, "Wee list not to declare,
Nor shew whose men wee bee.

"Yett wee will spend our deerest blood
Thy cheefest harts to slay."
Then Douglas swore a solempne oathe,
And thus in rage did say;

"Ere thus I will outbraved bee,
One of us tow shall dye!
I know thee well! an Erle thou art,
Lord Percy! Soe am I;

"But trust me, Percye, pittye it were,
And great offence, to kill
Then any of these our guiltlesse men,
For they have done none ill;

"Let thou and I the battell trye,
And set our men aside."
"Accurst bee he!" Erle Percy sayd,
"By whome it is denyed."

Then stept a gallant Squire forth, —
   Witherington was his name, —
Who said, "I wold not have it told
   To Henery our King, for shame,

"That ere my captaine fought on foote,
   And I stand looking on:
You bee two Erles," quoth Witherington,
   "And I a Squier alone,

"Ile doe the best that doe I may,
   While I have power to stand!
While I have power to weeld my sword,
   Ile fight with hart and hand!"

Our English archers bend their bowes —
   Their harts were good and trew, —
Att the first flight of arrowes sent,
   Full foure score Scotts they slew.

To drive the deere with hound and horne,
   Douglas bade on the bent;
Two captaines moved with mickle might
   Their speres to shivers went.

They closed full fast on everye side,
   Noe slacknes there was found,
But many a gallant gentleman
   Lay gasping on the ground.

O Christ! it was great greeve to see
  How eche man chose his spere,
And how the blood out of their brests
  Did gush like water cleare!

At last these two stout Erles did meet
  Like captaines of great might;
Like Lyons wood they layd on lode,
  They made a cruell fight.

They fought untill they both did sweat,
  With swords of tempered steele,
Till blood a-downe their cheekes like raine
  They trickling downe did feele.

"O yeeld thee, Percye!" Douglas sayd,
  And infaith I will thee bringe
Where thou shall high advanced bee
  By James our Scottish King;

"Thy ransome I will freely give,
  And this report of thee,
Thou art the most couragious Knight
  That ever I did see."

"Noe, Douglas!" quoth Erle Percy then,
  "Thy profer I doe scorne;
I will not yeelde to any Scott
  That ever yett was borne!"

With that there came an arrow keene
   Out of an English bow,
Who scorke Erle Douglas on the brest
   A deepe and deadlye blow;

Who never sayd more words then these,
   "Fight on my merrymen all!
For why, my life is att an end,
   Lord Percy sees my fall."

Then leaving liffe, Erle Percy tooke
   The dead man by the hand;
And said, "Erle Douglas! for thy sake
   Wold I had lost my land!

"O Christ! my verry hart doth bleed
   For sorrow for thy sake!
For sure, a more redoubted Knight,
   Mischance cold never take!"

PART II

A KNIGHT amongst the Scotts there was,
   Which saw Erle Douglas dye,
Who streight in hart did vow revenge
   Upon the Lord Percye.

Sir Hugh Mountgomerye was he called,
   Who, with a spere full bright,
Well mounted on a gallant steed,
   Ran feircly through the fight,

And past the English archers all
　　Without all dread or feare,
And through Erle Percyes body then
　　He thrust his hatfull spere,

With such a vehement force and might,
　　That his body he did gore,
The staff ran through the other side
　　A large cloth yard and more.

Thus did both those nobles dye,
　　Whose courage none cold staine,
An English archer then perceived
　　The noble Erle was slaine,

He had a good bow in his hand
　　Made of a trusty tree;
An arrow of a cloth yard long
　　To the hard head haled hee,

Against Sir Hugh Mountgomerye
　　His shaft full right he sett;
The grey goose winge that was there-on,
　　In his harts bloode was wett.

This fight from breake of day did last
　　Till setting of the sun,
For when they rung the Evening bell
　　The battele scarse was done.

With stout Erle Percy there was slaine
   Sir John of Egerton,
Sir Robert Harcliffe and Sir William,
   Sir James that bold barron;

And with Sir George and Sir James,
   Both Knights of good account;
And good Sir Raphe Rebbye there was
     slaine,
   Whose prowesse did surmount.

For Witherington needs must I wayle
   As one in doleful dumpes,
For when his leggs were smitten of,
   He fought upon his stumpes.

And with Erle Douglas there was slaine
   Sir Hugh Mountgomerye,
And Sir Charles Morrell that from feelde
   One foote wold never flee;

Sir Roger Hever of Harcliffe tow, —
   His sisters sonne was hee, —
Sir David Lamb so well esteemed
   But saved he cold not bee;

And the Lord Maxwell in like case
   With Douglas he did dye;
Of twenty hundred Scottish speeres,
   Scarce fifty five did flye;

Of fifteen hundred Englishmen
  Went home but fifty three;
The rest in Chevy-Chase were slaine,
  Under the greenwoode tree.

Next day did many widdowes come
  Their husbands to bewayle;
They washt their wounds in brinish teares,
  But all wold not prevayle.

Theyr bodyes bathed in purple blood,
  They bore with them away,
They kist them dead a thousand times
  Ere they were cladd in clay.

The newes was brought to Eddenborrow
  Where Scottland's King did rayne,
That brave Erle Douglas soddainlye
  Was with an arrow slaine.

"O heavy newes!" King James can say,
  "Scottland may wittenesse bee
I have not any captaine more
  Of such account as hee!"

Like tydings to King Henery came
  Within as short a space,
That Percy of Northumberland
  Was slaine in Chevy-Chase.

'Now God be with him!" said our King,
  "Sith it will noe better bee,
I trust I have within my realme
  Five hundred as good as hee!

"Yett shall not Scotts nor Scottland say
  But I will vengeance take,
And be revenged on them all
  For brave Erle Percyes sake."

This vow the King did well performe
  After on Humble Downe;
In one day fifty Knights were slayne,
  With Lords of great renowne,

And of the rest of small account,
  Did many hundreds dye:
Thus endeth the hunting in Chevy-Chase
  Made by the Erle Percye.

God save our King, and blesse this land
  With plentye, joy, and peace;
And grant hencforth that foule debate
  Twixt noble men may ceaze!

ffins.

THE BALLAD OF MEIKLE-MOUTHED MEG

BOLD WILLIE SCOTT

THE moonbeam glints on tower and hill,
　It's hey! for the bonny moonlight!
"Go saddle my steed, I'll ride betimes,
　The English Border to-night."

"Take tent, good lad, the Warder's men
　Are riding over the land."
"Tuts! six Scotts lads will keep two score
　Of such feckless loons at a stand!"

Oh! they were twenty stout and bold,
　Mounted on active naigs;
Some armed wi' guns and Jeddart staves,
　Wi' iron round their craigs.

Young Scott o' Harden, led them on
　To the lands o' Elibank;
"Good faith, I wat Sir Gideon
　Will no his kindness thank."

He left his towers by Ettrick's stream,
　His minnie's proverb scorning;
When Scotts set foot in the stirrup-ring,
　The blood will flow ere morning.

Sir Gideon and young Willie Scott
  Were ever deadly foes;
Ere they shall clasp each other's hand,
  The Gowan shall grow on the Rose.

THE RAID

THEY gained the lands o' Elibank,
  And gathered the gear together;
They counted tens, and came to scores,
  And drove them out the heather.

There was not a Murray on the lea,
  Young Scott his heart was light;
"There'll be a dry breakfast at Elibank,
  At Oakwood, a meal to-night."

They got half way to Ettrick stream,
  When they heard a sleuth-hound yell,
And Scott well kenned his mortal foe,
  Pursued him o'er the fell.

Sir Gideon was a doure fierce man,
  A terror to a foe;
He had a wife and daughters three,
  Well dowered they were I trow.

He let young Harden steal his cows,
  And, oh! his arm was slack;
But the grim old Knight was looking on
  Wi' fifty men at his back.

"I have thee now like a thief in a mill,"
　Sir Gideon o' Elibank said;
He gave the word to loose the hounds;
　And the hot pursuit he led.

"Young Scott, yield quietly to me,"
　Sir Gideon loudly cried,
"Or a thief's death shall ye die,
　If ye the onset bide.

"Ye've driven off my cows and sheep,
　And byre and fold are toom,
The corbies and ye shall be acquaint,
　For what this night ye've done."

"Brag on! brag on! ye old greybeard!
　While Scott o' Harden stands,
No power on earth shall make him yield
　To any o' Murray's bands.

"So do your best, and do your worst,
　Here's a hand and sword to fight;
I trow a Scott ne'er turned his back
　Whilst a Murray was in sight."

"Small mercy after what ye've stol'n,
　I had designed for thee;
But, callant, after what ye've said,
　I'll prove your enemy."

"Thou old man, measure weapons then,
　And I would have ye leave
Your well-faured daughters to the world,
　For your loss must they grieve."

"Before sunrise," quoth Gideon,
　"You'll speak less vauntingly;
Say what ye like of me, you dog,
　But leave my bairnies be."

The strife went high and bloodily,
　They grappled at the throat;
And many was the Elibank,
　The reavers deadly smote.

The guns banged off, the sleuth-hounds yelled,
　The cattle rowted sore;
And many wights lay on the ground,
　That up rose never more.

The fray went hard wi' Willie Scott,
　His horse fell wi' a bound,
And many Murrays wi' their swords
　Bore him unto the ground.

THE GALLOWS OR MARRIAGE

LADY MURRAY came forth at noon,
　To welcome her husband home;
And there she spied young Scott o' Harden,
　All bounden and his lone.

They thrust the Scott in a darksome **room,**
  And left him to his thought;
But neither bread nor yet red wine
  Unto the youth they brought.

"And what, Lord Gideon," said his **dame,**
  "Will ye do wi' young Scott?"
"Do ye see yonder branch o' the elm,
  For that shall be his lot."

"O goodman," quo' his pitying dame,
  "Ye could not do this thing;
For lifting a pickle o' your nowt,
  So brave a lad to hing!"

"What mercy did ever a Scott o' **them**
  E'er show to me or mine?
The reaving Scotts shall surely **weep,**
  The last of all their line."

She said, "But we have daughters **three,**
  And they are no well-faured,
When ye've a husband to your **hand,**
  To hang him would be hard."

"Sooth, goodwife, faith, but ye are **right!**
  There's wisdom in your say;
This birkie Scott shall have his **choice,**
  To wed what one he may.

"We'll give him respite to the morn,
    Nor hang him 'gainst all law;
To marry our daughter Meikle-Mouthed Meg,
    Or choke with the death-thraw."

Quo' she, " To marry our daughter Meg
    More wiselike would it be,
Than kill the hope of an old, old House
    And strap him to the tree."

Quo' he, " If I were in his place,
    I would refuse I ween,
And die a death upon the tree,
    Than wed what I'd ne'er seen.

"Go ye, and tell our daughter Meg,
    That she's be wived the morn;
And I will to this young gallant,
    And see what he perform."
    .   .   .   .   .   .

She went unto her daughter Meg,
    Who had a meikle mouth;
But her teeth were pearls, and her honey breath
    Was like the wind from the South.

The mother sat by her daughter's side;
    "Sweet Meg, come tell me this,
Wouldst thou the rather be a bride,
    Then live in singleness?

"Before I was your age, I trow,
  I was in a bride her place."
"Aye, mother," quo' Meg, and sighed full sore,
  "But ye had a well-faured face.

"But you shall see the Ettrick stream
  Run thro' the dells o' Yarrow,
Before ye hear o' an offer to me,
  Or a man to be my marrow.

"My face is foul, my heart is large,
  A kinder none there is;
And must I pass away my days,
  In sullen loneliness?"

The mother told her of young Scott,
  And waited her reply;
"O Mother, I'd rather marry him
  Than ever he should die!"

But the tears rose welling from their spring,
  And filled her cushat eyes;
"But, Mother, how if when we're wed,
  He should my heart despise?"

"Oh, marriage," quo' the wily dame,
  "Is not that hard to snoove,
If ye should marry Willie Scott,
  Ye'll be like hand and glove."

.   ʻ   .   .   .   .   .

Sir Gideon entered young Scott's dungeon;
  "Thy death is at my hand,
Ye came as a thief in the dead o' night,
  And stole my cows from my land.

"But I'll give ye a chance for life,
  For all ye have said of me,
Either to marry my daughter Meg,
  Or hang upon yonder tree.

"And the boldest Scott on the **Border March,**
  Shall never take ye down,
Until your skeleton is seen
  And ye drop away bone by bone."

"And ye would spare my life," he said,
  "For all ye come so gleg,
If I would stoop and give my hand
  To your bonny daughter Meg?

"Ye are the Murray of Elibank,
  I Scott of Oakwood Tower,
I would not marry your daughter **Meg,**
  Tho' a kingdom were her dower;

"But little I fear to meet my death,
  As I do to tell you this;
An ye had fallen in my hands,
  Such were your fate, I wiss.

"Ye think that your winsome daughter Meg,"
   Oh! he spoke so scornfully, —
"Will get a husband at the last,
   But, faith, my lad, ye lie,

"I rather choose upon the gallows
   To render up my breath;
I trow there will be Scots enough
   Left to revenge my death."

"There is my thumb, thou young braggart,"
   Sir Gideon chafing cried,
"I would n't hinder ye your choice
   For death shall be your bride.

"And let the Scots o' a' the Border
   Revenge your death that dare."
He left young Scott unto himself,
   And quit his dungeon stair.

YOUNG WILLIE'S MESSENGER

It was about the midnight time,
   When his dungeon door ga'ed back;
And the sentinel who guarded it
   Let in a woman in black.

"What want ye wi' me, fair Maiden?"
   The Scott o' Harden said.
"I come to ask if thy dying wish
   Can be by me obeyed?

" I am a lassie o' the house,
    And wait on Sir Gideon's dame;
And tho' ye have refused poor Meg,
    Her prayers will be the same."

"Why has Dame Murray sent thee here?" —
    "She has a woman's heart.
Ye have a mother and sisters twain,
    From whom full soon ye part.

"If ye have anything to say,
    Ye would have carried there,
I swear by all that's good on earth,
    To be your messenger."

"Maiden," quo' he, and his voice was low,
    "Of my mother do not speak;
I wish to die as my father's son,
    And yet her heart I break."

"It cannot be," then said the girl,
    "Ye have rejected Meg,
Without the looking on her face?
    I'm sure your life she'd beg."

"I have not seen, but I have heard
    Her face described to me;
And, by my faith, between the two,
    I'll chose the gallows-tree."

The tears fell from that poor girl's eyes,
  In anger or in spleen? —
And ever and anon she sighed,
  And deep sobs came between.

"Belike," quo' she, " they've painted **her**
  Far worse than she may look;
Many a man has an ugly wife,
  That the gallows could not brook."

"I have no wish to see her **face,**
  Far less to marry her;
But ye seem o' a kindly heart,
  And aiblins are as fair.

"So let me see your face, my **joy,**
  And by your countenance,
I'll see if I dare trust you with
  A letter for my chance?"

She threw the veil from off her **face,**
  "I'm no well faured I know;
But kernels lie inside hard shells,
  And gold in the earth below."

"So sweet and sensible ye speak,
  Ye almost make me wish,
Meikle-Mouthed Meg was like **to you,**
  So kind, so young, so lish. '

He held the light within the cruse
   Close to the maiden's face,
Wi' loof o'er e'en, he earnestly
   Perused each simple grace.

He saw her face was fair and round,
   Her lips like a large rose-leaf;
And her snow-white teeth so even **showed,**
   Like ivory from their sheath.

There stood a tear in her dove-blue eye,
   Her eye so mild and meek,
A large tear slowly left the lid,
   And trickled down her cheek.

"Ye have the lock that never lied,
   And tho' no fine your face,
Ye've pleasing sense and kindliness
   Wi' every modest grace.

"So bring to me the writing ink,
   The paper and pen so fine;
And tho' ye abide wi' my enemy,
   Ye'll take my mother a line."

She rolled it up so carefully,
   The letter he writ so fair;
She had no silk, but she tied it with
   A lock o' her golden hair.

THE GALLOWS-TREE

It was by cock-crowing the morn,
  When Meg wi' crippled feet,
Like one that had a long way walked
  Came in, her sire to greet.

"Grant me another day," she cried,
  "For young Willie Scott his life;
And throw not by the chance, your **Meg**
  Has to become a wife."

Sir Gideon rubbed his hands in glee,
  "I grant it for your sake;
But if he then refuse your hand,
  He shall his own way take."

Much wondered the Laird o' Oakwood **Tower,**
  As fell the evening gloom,
They did not hang him in the morn,
  As he had heard his doom.

He heard the sentry shoot the bolt,
  And a kind o' murmuring;
And then his mother and sisters two
  Wi' loud outcries break in.

And, "O my Son!" the mother cried,
  "Is there no other way,
To save thee from a cruel death,
  At the hands o' a fierce Murray?

"Marry his daughter, Willie dear,
　And save thy mother's life;
Tho' she be ugly — what of that?
　She'll make a frugal wife."

"Mother, I will not take his terms.
　Who brought ye here?" he said.
"Who, but your messenger so good,
　That kind and sonsy maid."

They passed the time in grief and woe,
　Throughout the dead of night;
Nor ever they ceased to weep wi' him,
　Until the morning's light.

The loud horn blew out o'er the lea,
　Sir Gideon stood him before;
"What is thy choice, young man?" he cried,
　"Or ere this deed be o'er."

"The gallows still before the wife,"
　Young Harden stoutly said.
"And wi' the hemp around my throat,
　I'll spit on the ground ye tread."

They led him forth to the gallows-tree;
　When he saw that maiden there,
Who at her risk, unto his mother
　Carried his last letter;

The thoughts o' the gallows could not stir
  The heart o' that dauntless Chief,
But the weeping look of that young girl,
  It pierced his soul wi' grief.

And while the tear hung in her eye,
  He took her lily hand;
And said, " Thy heart is far too meek,
  For such a ruffian band.

"Hear me, Murray, speak my mind,
  I care not for thy word,
I'd rather marry this poor maiden,
  If should my life be spared,

"Then ever I'd wed thy daughter Meg." —
  Sir Gideon clapped his hand;
"A bargain! I take thee at thy word,
  Young Scott where dost thou stand."

  .   .   .   .

They buckled them in holy bonds,
  The priest he prayed the while;
And when the marriage knot was tied,
  Sir Gideon blithe did smile.

His mother fell upon his neck,
  "God bless my bairn, he's free!
And bless the bonny lassie yet,
  Who brought the word to me!"

"I give thee a father's blessing, sir,"
   The Murray blithely cried;
"For what?" — The lassie modest said,
   "Meikle-Mouthed Meg's your bride."

Oh! then sore shame fell on the Scott,
   And tears came in his eyes;
"And is my bride the scorned Meg,
   That I did so despise?

"Let no man hate what he's not seen,
   The shame on me doth lay: —
I rose this morning for my death,
   And it ends in my bridal day!"

                (Englished. Condensed)

BELTED WILL

THE ROBBER BARON

THE Baron of Thirlwall came from the wars,
   Laden with treasure bold;
Among the which a fair table,
   All of the beaten gold.

And men will speak of the Baron's wealth,
   Whatever he may say,
And how a grizzly Dwarf does guard
   His treasure night and day.

Many a Border freebooter
   Eyed Thirlwall's good Castle,
Thinking to win the bags of gold,
   And eke the fair table.

But the Baron hath retainers bold,
   And swatchers many ane,
And the Castle walls are high to win,
   Howe'er they fidge and fain.

The boldest one o' a' his men,
   Was Jockey of the Sheugh;
The Baron loved him like a brother,
   And that was fair enoo.

Jock could wrestle, run, or leap,
   Wi' ever a living man;
Never a wight in Cumbernauld
   Could beat him at the span.

But Thirlwall's Baron heeded not
   The word o' Belted Will,
Who dwells within the dark Naworth,
   The Border March to still;

He can rule all the Border round,
   Wi' a peeled willow-wand;
But Thirlwall's Baron gecks at him,
   And all the laws o' the land

So fast come tidings of ravin wrong
   To Belted Willy's ear;
Quo' he, "By my belt, I'll trap this man,
   If I catch him in effeir.

"But he is like a wily fox,
   That taketh to his hole,
An I can catch him on the turn,
   I'll smoke him from his bole.

"He reaves and harrows every one,
   Tho' he has goups o' gold;
I'll lay a trap for him bedeen,
   By which he shall be sold."

Thirlwall's Baron heard his speech,
   Wi' scorn almost he burst;
"His anger it is like a haggis,
   That's hottest at the first."

Sore smiled the wily Belted Will,
   But in so dark a way;
Better that smile were wanting there,
   Than on his lip to lay.

THE TRAP O' BELTED WILL

JOCK o' the Sheugh tirled at the string,
   Of the Baron of Thirlwall's yett;
"Up, up, and rise, my noble Lord,
   Some plunder for to get.

"There are a swatch o' Englishers
    Coming from Carlysle town,
Well laden wi' the yellow gold,
    For Annan are they boun'."

"Go, take a dozen o' my men,
    And brattle o'er the lea,
Lay wait, and watch until they pass
    The Bowness Witches' Tree.

"A dozen o' ye well may lick
    Three score o' English tikes,
Take all they have, and leave them so
    To tell o' this who likes."

Then Jock banged o'er the broomy knoll,
    And reached the Witches' Tree,
And wi' his dozen freebooters,
    Lay down on their bellie.

There came on twenty Englishers,
    Wi' cloaks and saddlebags;
There came on twenty travellers,
    Mounted on goodly nags.

Came on those twenty travellers,
    With long cloaks flowing down,
Came on these twenty travellers,
    All thro' the yellow broom.

Then started up Jock and his men
  Wi' such an awful yell,
Ye might have heard it at the top
  Of Skiddaw or Criffell.

"Come off your nags, ye sorning crew,
  Of Southron pock-puddings,
Or ye shall have the good cold steel,
  So give us all your things!"

"We'll give ye that," said one o' them,
  "Ye'll no forget, I wiss,
This many a day, good Jock o' the Sheugh,
  And that my billie's this!"

They threw the cloaks from off their hides,
  And back and breastplate shone;
They grippit their swords, the first blow struck
  Was echoed with a groan.

Good faith! but Jock had found his match,
  For the Southrons hacked about;
The Thirlwall boys were fain to fight,
  But soon put to the route.

Of twelve o' Jock's good freebooters,
  But three fled o'er the lea,
The other nine lay still enough
  Beside the Witches' Tree.

Poor Jock is down upon his back,
  Wi' a fair clour on the head;
His billies all are stiffening,
  And three o' them are fled.

Out spoke the twenty travellers,
  "Why, Jock, how's this of a',
Ye bid us to a meal, good faith,
  And then ye run awa'?"

Quo' Jock, as they bound fast his arms,
  And raised him from the lea,
"If I had kenned ye were Belted Will's men,
  The Devil might stopped ye for me!"

THE GRIZZLY DWARF

THE Baron o' Thirlwall looked abroad,
  From out his strong Castle,
And he saw three men come posting on,
  Out o'er the fern and fell.

"I wad," said he, "they run a race,
  A thousand merks I lay
Upon the wight in the red jerkin,
  He wins the race this day."

The three men burst in on his room,
  "My Lord," then each one said,
"Jock o' the Sheugh is wounded fair,
  And nine good fellows dead."

The dark spot flew to the Baron's cheek,
  "Ye cowards, one and all!
Go, join your bloody billies then,
  Whatever may befall!"

He struck each man the neck intil,
  And they fell on the floor;
"To fly without a single blow,
  Shows valour to be poor!

"If Belted Will should harm a hair
  O' Jock o' the Sheugh his head,
I'll put the Border in such a blaze,
  Shall make him flee with dread.

"If Jock o' the Sheugh hangs for this play,
  The whole of the March shall weep,
No man shall waken in the morn,
  That goes alive to sleep."

They brought these words to Belted Will
  As at racket-ball he played;
But the only answer he let fall,
  "We'll soon see that," he said.

    .   .   .   .

By Brampton's town there stands an oak,
  Upon a hill so high;
And Jock was broughten there betimes
  Upon the tree to die.

They strapped him to the highest branch
  Of all that goodly tree;
And there the righteous chaplain prayed
  For Jock's soul solemnlie,

Thirlwall's Baron saw the sight,
  And swore revenge to have;
For better part o' a summer's day
  He nothing did but rave.

He sent a messenger so bold
  To Will, who cried in scorn,
"Better he looks unto his nest,
  I'll burn it ere the morn!"

The Baron fled to his Castle,
  And guarded it so grim,
"The fiend take Belted Will," he cried,
  "'T is word and blow wi' him."

But scarcely had the midnight fell,
  When spite o' a' his care,
Belted Will his Castle stormed,
  For a' he fought so fair.

A tar barrel and reeking peat,
  They laid unto his nest,
Threw open gates and wide windows,
  And the night wind did the rest.

The Baron fled from room to room,
  By the flames of his own hall,
"He's gi'en me light to go to bed,
  Whatever may befall."

He rushed into his inner room,
  Where his golden table lay;
The Devil in likeness o' a Dwarf
  Kept watch there night and day.

Belted Will pursued him hard,
  Amid the flame and stour,
For he cut the skirt from the Baron's cloak,
  As he whiskèd through the door.

"Save me, now, thou gruesome Elf,
  And my soul and body's thine!"
The Dwarf he jabbered hideously,
  But never made a sign.

Belted Will called for a ram,
  To bash the doorway down;
The red flames thro' the keyhole flashed,
  And filled wi' reek the room.

"My soul and body," the Baron said,
  Abjuring Christ His sign;
The Devil he grippit him in his arms,
  "Now, Baron, art thou mine."

The door ga'ed splintering from the posts,
　In rushed the enemy;
But Baron, Dwarf, and gold table,
　I wat they could ne'er see.

And legends say the ugsome Dwarf
　Threw all into a well,
And by the glamour o' his art
　Cast over all a spell;

Which never may be rendered vain
　But by a Widow's Son;
And he shall find the gold table,
　When years away have run.

Frederick Sheldon. (Condensed)

BRAVE HEARTS AND PROUD

EARL HALDAN'S DAUGHTER

A.D. 1400

It was Earl Haldan's daughter,
She looked across the sea;
She looked across the water,
And long and loud laughed she:
"The locks of six Princesses
Must be my marriage-fee,
So hey bonny boat, and ho bonny boat!
Who comes a-wooing me!"

It was Earl Haldan's daughter,
She walked along the sand;
When she was aware of a Knight so fair,
Come sailing to the land.
His sails were all of velvet,
His mast of beaten gold,
And "hey bonny boat, and ho bonny boat,
Who saileth here so bold?"

"The locks of five Princesses
I won beyond the sea;
I shore their golden tresses,
To fringe a cloak for thee.
One handful yet is wanting,
But one of all the tale;
So hey bonny boat, and ho bonny boat!
Furl up thy velvet sail!"

He leapt into the water,
That rover young and bold;
He gript Earl Haldan's daughter,
He shore her locks of gold;
"Go weep, go weep, proud Maiden,
The tale is full to-day.
Now hey bonny boat, and ho bonny boat!
Sail Westward ho, and away!"

Charles Kingsley

LADY CLARE

It was the time when lilies blow,
   And clouds are highest up in air,
Lord Ronald brought a lily-white doe
   To give his cousin, Lady Clare.

I trow they did not part in scorn;
   Lovers long-betrothed were they;
They two will wed the morrow morn —
   God's blessing on the day!

"He does not love me for my birth,
   Nor for my lands so broad and fair;
He loves me for my own true worth,
   And that is well," said Lady Clare.

In there came old Alice the nurse,
   Said, "Who was this that went from thee?"
"It was my cousin," said Lady Clare;
   "To-morrow he weds with me."

"O God be thanked!" said Alice the nurse,
   "That all comes round so just and fair!
Lord Ronald is heir of all your lands,
   And you are *not* the Lady Clare."

"Are ye out of your mind, my Nurse, my Nurse,"
Said Lady Clare, "that ye speak so wild?"
"As God's above," said Alice the nurse,
"I speak the truth: you are my child.

"The old Earl's daughter died at my breast;
I speak the truth, as I live by bread!
I buried her like my own sweet child,
And put my child in her stead."

"Falsely, falsely have ye done,
O Mother," she said, "if this be true,
To keep the best man under the sun
So many years from his due."

"Nay now, my Child," said Alice the nurse,
"But keep the secret for your life,
And all you have will be Lord Ronald's
When you are man and wife."

"If I'm a beggar born," she said,
"I will speak out, for I dare not lie.
Pull off, pull off, the brooch of gold,
And fling the diamond necklace by."

"Nay now, my Child," said Alice the nurse,
"But keep the secret all ye can."
She said, "Not so; but I will know
If there be any faith in man."

"Nay now, what faith?" said Alice the nurse;
  "The man will cleave unto his right."
"And he shall have it," the lady replied,
  "Tho' I should die to-night."

"Yet give one kiss to your mother dear!
  Alas, my Child, I sinned for thee!"
"O Mother, Mother, Mother," she said,
  "So strange it seems to me.

"Yet here's a kiss for my mother dear,
  My mother dear, if this be so,
And lay your hand upon my head,
  And bless me, Mother, ere I go."

She clad herself in a russet gown,
  She was no longer Lady Clare;
She went by dale, and she went by down,
  With a single rose in her hair.

The lily-white doe Lord Ronald had brought
  Leapt up from where she lay,
Dropt her head in the maiden's hand,
  And followed her all the way.

Down stept Lord Ronald from his tower:
  "O Lady Clare, you shame your worth!
Why come you drest like a village maid,
  That are the flower of the earth?"

"If I come drest like a village maid,
  I am but as my fortunes are;
I am a beggar born," she said,
  "And not the Lady Clare."

"Play me no tricks," said Lord Ronald,
  "For I am yours in word and in deed.
"Play me no tricks," said Lord Ronald,
  "Your riddle is hard to read."

Oh, and proudly stood she up!
  Her heart within her did not fail;
She looked into Lord Ronald's eyes,
  And told him all her nurse's tale.

He laughed a laugh of merry scorn;
  He turned, and kissed her where she stood;
"If you are not the heiress born,
  And I," said he, "the next in blood, —

"If you are not the heiress born,
  And I," said he, "the lawful heir,
We two will wed to-morrow morn,
  And you shall still be Lady Clare."
              Alfred, Lord Tennyson

PROUD LADY MARGARET

FAIR MARGRET was a young ladye,
  An come of high degree;
Fair Margret was a young ladye,
  An proud as proud coud be.

Fair Margret was a rich ladye,
  The king's cousin was she;
Fair Margaret was a rich ladye,
  An vain as vain coud be.

She war'd her wealth on the gay cleedin
  That comes frae yont the sea,
She spent her time frae morning till night
  Adorning her fair bodye.

Ae night she sate in her stately ha,
  Kaimin her yellow hair,
When in there cum like a gentle knight,
  An a white scarf he did wear.

"O what's your will wi me, sir knight,
  O what's your will wi me?
You're the likest to my ae brother
  That ever I did see.

"You're the likest to my ae brother
  That ever I hae seen,
But he's buried in Dunfermline kirk,
  A month an mair bygane."

"I'm the likest to your ae brother
  That ever ye did see,
But I canna get rest into my grave,
  A' for the pride of thee.

"Leave pride, Margret, leave pride, Margret,
  Leave pride an vanity;
Ere ye see the sights that I hae seen,
  Sair altered ye maun be.

"O ye come in at the kirk-door
  Wi the gowd plaits in your hair;
But wud ye see what I hae seen,
  Ye maun them a' forbear.

"O ye come in at the kirk-door
  Wi the gowd prins i your sleeve;
But wad ye see what I hae seen,
  Ye maun gie them a' their leave.

"Leave pride, Margret, leave pride, Margret,
  Leave pride an vanity;
Ere ye see the sights that I hae seen,
  Sair altered ye maun be."

He got her in her stately ha,
  Kaimin her yellow hair,
He left her on her sick sick bed,
  Sheding the saut saut tear.

THE FAMOUS FLOWER OF SERVING-MEN

PART I

You beautious ladies, great and small,
I write unto you one and all,
Whereby that you may understand
What I have suffered in this land.

I was by birth a lady fair,
My father's chief and onely heir,
But when my good old father dy'd,
Then was I made a young knight's bride.

And then my love built me a bower,
Bedeckt with many a fragrant flower;
A braver bower you never did see
Then my true-love did build for me.

But there came thieves late in the night,
They rob'd my bower, and slew my knight,
And after that my knight was slain,
I could no longer there remain.

My servants all from me did flye,
In the midst of my extremity,
And left me by my self alone,
With a heart more cold then any stone.

Yet, though my heart was full of care,
Heaven would not suffer me to despair;
Wherefore in hast I chang'd my name
From Fair Elise to Sweet William.

And therewithal I cut my hair,
And drest my self in man's attire,
My doublet, hose, and bever-hat,
And a golden band about my neck.

With a silver rapier by my side,
So like a gallant I did ride;
The thing that I delighted on,
Was for to be a serving-man.

Thus in my sumptuous man's array
I bravely rode along the way;
And at the last it chanced so
That I unto the king's court did go.

Then to the king I bowed full low,
My love and duty for to show,
And so much favour I did crave
That I a serving-man's place might have.

"Stand up, brave youth," the king replyd,
"Thy service shall not be denyd;
But tell me first what thou canst do;
Thou shalt be fitted thereunto.

"Wilt thou be usher of my hall,
To wait upon my nobles all?
Or wilt thou be taster of my wine,
To wait on me when I shall dine?

"Or wilt thou be my chamberlain,
To make my bed both soft and fine?
Or wilt thou be one of my guard?
And I will give thee thy reward."

Sweet William, with a smiling face,
Said to the king, "If 't please your grace
To show such favour unto me,
Your chamberlain I fain would be."

The king then did the nobles call,
To ask the counsel of them all,
Who gave consent Sweet William he
The king's own chamberlain should be.

PART II

Now mark what strange things came to pass:
As the king one day a hunting was,
With all his lords and noble train,
Sweet William did at home remain.

Sweet William had no company then
With him at home but an old man;
And when he saw the coast was clear,
He took a lute which he had there.

Upon the lute Sweet William plaid,
And to the same he sung and said,
With a pleasant and most noble voice,
Which made the old man to rejoyce:

My father was as brave a lord
As ever Europe did afford;
My mother was a lady bright,
My husband was a valiant knight.

And I my self a lady gay,
Bedeckt with gorgeous rich array;
The bravest lady in the land
Had not more pleasures to command.

I had my musick every day,
Harmonious lessons for to play;
I had my virgins fair and free,
Continually to wait on me.

But now, alas! my husband's dead,
And all my friends are from me fled;
My former joys are past and gone,
For now I am a serving-man.

At last the king from hunting came,
And presently upon the same
He called for the good old man,
And thus to speak the king began.

"What news, what news, old man?" quod he;
"What news hast thou to tell to me?"
"Brave news," the old man he did say;
"Sweet William is a lady gay."

"If this be true thou tellest me
I 'le make thee a lord of high degree;
But if thy words do prove a lye,
Thou shalt be hanged up presently."

But when the king the truth had found,
His joys did more and more abound;
According as the old man did say,
Sweet William was a lady gay.

Therefore the king without delay
Put on her glorious rich array,
And upon her head a crown of gold,
Which was most famous to behold.

And then, for fear of further strife,
He took Sweet William for his wife;
The like before was never seen,
A serving-man to be a queen.

COCHRANE'S BONNY GRIZZY

PART I

LISTEN, now, both great and simple,
    Whilst I croon to you my song,
Ere such another damsel 'pears,
    The world will cease to wag ere long:
For she is the flower o'er all the bower,
My blessings on Cochrane's Bonny Grizzy!

Her father lay long in the Embro jail,
    Wearing fast to his end,
For his head must be swept clean from his shoul-
        ders,
    When the warrant the King shall send;
Singing "Woes me!" wi' the tear in her e'e,
Did Cochrane's bonny daughter mourn!

She kissed her father's lyart locks,
    Unkempt for many a day,
And she said, "To save my father's life,
    I aiblins ken a way:
Give me thy love, that I fortune prove?"
Quo' Cochrane's bonny daughter!

She rode away thro' the stragglling town,
    Of beggart Hadingtown,
Syne by Dunbar, thro' Coppersmith,
    Till to Berwick she has come:

And she rapped right loud on the barred gates,
Did Cochrane's bonny daughter!

She slept all night and she rose betimes,
   And crossed the long bridge of the Tweed;
And over the moor at Tweedmouth brae,
   Sore draggit was her woman's weed;
And lightin' down by Haggerston Shaws,
Did Cochrane's Bonny Grizzy!

A cloak she drew from her saddlebag,
   With trunks and a doublet fair;
She cut off with a folding knife,
   Her long and raven hair;
And she dressed herself in laddie's clothes,
Did Cochrane's Bonny Grizzy!

The horseman rode into Belford town,
   Who carried the London mail,
Bold Grizzy she sought tne hostel out,
   And there with a couthy tale,
Forgathered with the London Post,
Did Cochrane's Bonny Grizzy!

She roared the loudest of them a',
   Quo' the fellow, "My canty chiel,
Deil blaw my pipes! yere the crack o' the wa',
   And the best amang the hail!"
In the dead of night did they go to their beds,
And so did Cochrane's daughter!

She rose over the bed ere the second cock,
    Went jimply along the floor;
She's stown her father's death warrant,
    Whilst the lubber loud did snore.
She's gained the hills ere the hue and cry
They raised on Cochrane's daughter!

PART II

BUT the King can write another brief,
    For all the first be stown;
And once again the fellow rode,
    With the warrant from London town.
Now out and alas! What can she do?
For the heart of Grizzy sank!

The red sun went down o'er the sea,
    And the wind blew stiff and snell,
And as it shot by Grizzy's lugs,
    It sounded old Cochrane's knell.
"But downa despair, 't is a kittle carle!"
Said Cochrane's Bonny daughter!

The larch and the tall fir shrieked with pain,
    As they bent before the wind,
And down there fell the heavy rain,
    Till sense and eyes were blind;
"A lang night 't is ne'er sees a day,"
Quo' Cochrane's undaunted Grizzy!

The Warlocks are dancing threesome reels,
   On Goswick's haunted links,
The red fire shoots by Ladythorne,
   And Tam wi' the Lanthorne falls and sinks.
On Kyloe's hills there's awful sounds,
But they frighted not Cochrane's Grizzy!

The moon beams shot from the troubled sky,
   In glints of flickering light,
The horseman came skelping thro' the mire,
   For his mind was in affright:
His pistol cocked he held in his hand,
But the sient a fear had Grizzy!

As he came fornents the Fenwicke woods,
   From the whin-bushes shot out a flame;
His dappled filly reared up in affright,
   And backward over he came;
There's a hand on his craig, and a foot on
      his mouth,
'T was Cochrane's Bonny Grizzy!

"I will not take thy life," she said,
   "But give me thy London news;
No blood of thine shall syle my blad,
   Gin me ye dinna refuse:"
She's prie'd the warrant, and away she flew,
With the speed and strength of the wild curlew!

.   .   .   .

Love will make a foe grow kind,
    Love will bring blossom where bud is **naught,**
Love hath softened a kingly mind,
    Grizzy hath mercy to councillors taught.
Her friends at Court have prieven the life
O' Grizzy's banished father!

She's wedded unto a German Knight,
    Her bairnies blithe with her sire remain,
She's cast the laddie's clouts away,
    And her raven hair is growing again.
What think ye, gentles o' every degree,
Of Cochrane's Bonny Grizzy?

                              (*Englished*)

THE GREETING OF KYNAST

SHE said, "This narrow chamber is not for me
        the place,"
    Said the Lady Kunigunde of Kynast!
"'T is pleasanter on horseback, I'll hie me to the
        chase,"
    Said the Lady Kunigunde!

She said, "The Knight who weds me, I do require
        of him,"
    Said the Lady Kunigunde of Kynast!
"To gallop round the Kynast and break not neck
        nor limb."

A noble Knight came forward and galloped round
 the wall;
 The Lady Kunigunde of Kynast,
The lady without lifting a finger saw him fall.

And yet another galloped around the battlement;
 The Lady Kunigunde,
The lady saw him tumble, yet did she not relent.

And rider after rider spurred round his snorting
 horse;
 The Lady Kunigunde
Saw him vanish o'er the rampart, and never felt
 remorse.

Long time the folly lasted, then came no rider
 more;
 The Lady Kunigunde,
They would not ride to win her, the trial was too
 sore.

She stood upon her towers, she looked upon the
 land,
 The Lady Kunigunde of Kynast:
"I'm all alone at home here, will no one seek my
 hand?

"Is there none will ride to win me, to win me for
 his bride,
 The Lady Kunigunde of Kynast?

Oh fie! the paltry rider who dreads the bridal
    ride!''

Then out and spake from Thüringen the Land-
    grave Adelbert,
  ''The Lady Kunigunde of Kynast!
Well may the haughty damsel her worthiness as-
    sert.''

He trains his horse to gallop on narrow walls of
    stone;
  The Lady Kunigunde of Kynast!
''The lady shall not see us break neck or limb or
    bone.

''See here, O noble Lady, I'm he that dares the
    ride!''
  The Lady Kunigunde,
She looks in thoughtful silence, to see him sit in
    pride.

She saw him now make ready, then trembled she
    and sighed
  The Lady Kunigunde:
''Woe's me that I so fearful have made the bridal
    ride!''

Then rode he round the Kynast; her face she
    turned away,
  The Lady Kunigunde:

"Woe's me, the Knight is riding down to his
    grave to-day!"

He rides around the Kynast, right round the
    narrow wall;
  The Lady Kunigunde!
She cannot stir for terror her lily hand at all.

He rides around the Kynast, clear round the
    battlement;
  The Lady Kunigunde!
As if a breath might kill him, she held her breath
    suspent.

He rode around the Kynast and straight to her
    rode he;
  Said the Lady Kunigunde of Kynast:
"Thanks be to God in Heaven, who gave thy life
    to thee!

"Thanks be to God that into thy grave thou didst
    not ride!"
  Said the Lady Kunigunde:
"Come down from off thy horse now, O Knight,
    unto thy bride!"

Then spake the noble rider, and greeted, as he sate,
  The Lady Kunigunde:
"Oh, trust a Knight for horsemanship! well have
    I taught thee that.

"Now wait till comes another who can the same
        thing do,
  O Lady Kunigunde of Kynast!
I've wife and child already, can be no spouse
        for you!"

He gave his steed the spur, now; rode back the
        way he came;
  The Lady Kunigunde!
The lady saw him vanish, she swooned with scorn
        and shame.

And she remains a virgin, her pride had such a
        fall,
  The Lady Kunigunde!
Changed to a wooden image she stands in sight of
        all.

An image, like a hedgehog, with spines for hair,
        is now
  The Lady Kunigunde of Kynast!
The stranger has to kiss it, who climbs the Ky-
        nast's brow.

We bring it him to kiss it; and if it shocks his pride,
  The Lady Kunigunde Kynast!
He must pay down his forfeit, who will not kiss the
        bride,
  The Lady Kunigunde!

Charles T. Brooks, from Rückert

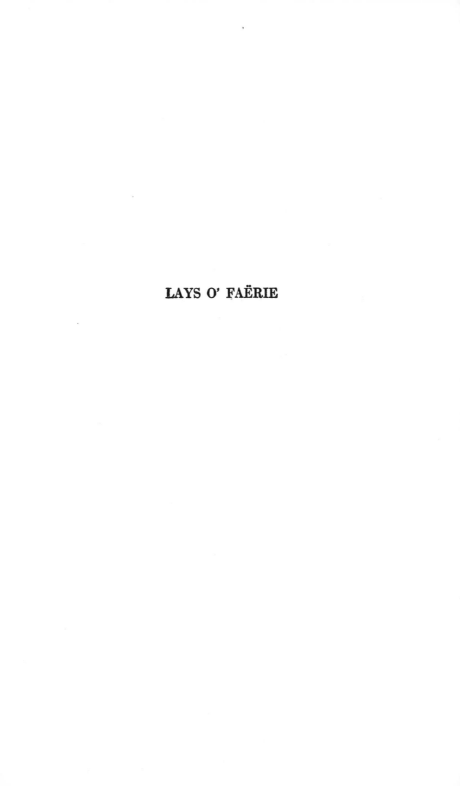

LAYS O' FAËRIE

THE FAIRY TEMPTER

A fair girl was sitting in the greenwood shade,
List'ning to the music the spring birds made;
When sweeter by far than the birds on the tree,
A voice murmured near her, "Oh! come, Love, with me —
        In earth or air,
        A thing so fair
      · *I have not seen as thee!*
        Then come, Love, with me."

"With a star for thy home, in a palace of light,
Thou wilt add a fresh grace to the beauty of night;
Or, if wealth be thy wish, thine are treasures untold,
I will show thee the birthplace of jewels and gold —
        And pearly caves
        Beneath the waves,
        All these, all these are thine,
        If thou wilt be mine."

Thus whispered a Fairy to tempt the fair girl,
But vain was his promise of gold and of pearl;
For she said, "Tho' thy gifts to a poor girl were dear,
My father, my mother, my sisters are here:
        Oh! what would be
        Thy gifts to me
        Of earth, and sea, and air,
        If my heart were not there?"

                          Samuel Lover

ALICE BRAND

I

MERRY it is in the good Greenwood,
  When the mavis and merle are singing,
When the deer sweeps by, and the hounds are
      in cry,
  And the hunter's horn is ringing.

"O Alice Brand, my native land
  Is lost for love of you;
And we must hold by wood and wold,
  As outlaws wont to do.

"O Alice, 't was all for thy locks so bright,
  And 't was all for thine eyes so blue,
That on the night of our luckless flight,
  Thy brother bold I slew.

"Now must I teach to hew the beech,
  The hand that held the glaive,
For leaves to spread our lowly bed,
  And stakes to fence our cave.

"And for vest of pall, thy fingers small,
  That wont on harp to stray,
A cloak must sheer from the slaughtered deer,
  To keep the cold away." —

"O Richard! if my brother died,
　'T was but a fatal chance;
For darkling was the battle tried,
　And fortune sped the lance.

"If pall and vair no more I wear,
　Nor thou the crimson sheen,
As warm, we'll say, is the russet grey,
　As gay the forest green.

"And, Richard, if our lot be hard,
　And lost thy native land,
Still Alice has her own Richard,
　And he his Alice Brand."

II

'T IS merry, 't is merry, in good Greenwood,
　So blithe Lady Alice is singing;
On the beech's pride, and oak's brown side,
　Lord Richard's axe is ringing.

Up spoke the moody Elfin King,
　Who woned within the hill, —
Like wind in the porch of a ruined church,
　His voice was ghostly shrill.

"Why sounds yon stroke on beech and oak,
　Our moonlight circle's screen?
Or who comes here to chase the deer,
　Beloved of our Elfin Queen?

Or who may dare on wold to wear
  The Fairies' fatal green?

"Up, Urgan, up! to yon mortal hie,
  For thou wert christened man;
For cross or sign thou wilt not fly,
  For muttered word or ban.

"Lay on him the curse of the withered heart,
  The curse of the sleepless eye;
Till he wish and pray that his life would part,
  Nor yet find leave to die."

III

'T is merry, 't is merry, in good Greenwood,
  Though the birds have stilled their singing;
The evening blaze doth Alice raise,
  And Richard is fagots bringing.

Up Urgan starts, that hideous Dwarf,
  Before Lord Richard stands,
And, as he crossed and blessed himself,
"I fear not sign," quoth the grisly Elf,
  "That is made with bloody hands."

But out then spoke she, Alice Brand
  That woman void of fear, —
"And if there's blood upon his hand,
  'T is but the blood of deer." —

"Now loud thou liest, thou bold of mood!
  It cleaves unto his hand,
The stain of thine own kindly blood,
  The blood of Ethert Brand."

Then forward stepped she, Alice Brand,
  And made the holy sign:
"And if there's blood on Richard's hand,
  A spotless hand is mine.

"And I conjure thee, Demon Elf,
  By Him whom Demons fear,
To show us whence thou art thyself,
  And what thine errand here?"

"'T is merry, 't is merry, in Fairyland,
  When Fairy Birds are singing,
When the Court doth ride by their Mon-
      arch's side,
  With bit and bridle ringing:

"And gaily shines the Fairyland —
  But all is glistening show,
Like the idle gleam that December's beam
  Can dart on ice and snow.

"And fading, like that varied gleam,
  Is our inconstant shape,
Who now like Knight and Lady seem,
  And now like Dwarf and Ape.

"It was between the night and day,
  When the Fairy King has power,
That I sunk down in a sinful fray,
And 'twixt life and death, was snatched away
  To the joyless Elfin Bower.

"But wist I of a woman bold,
  Who thrice my brow durst sign,
I might regain my mortal mould,
  As fair a form as thine."

She crossed him once, she crossed him twice —
  That Lady was so brave;
The fouler grew his goblin hue,
  The darker grew the cave.

She crossed him thrice, that Lady bold;
  He rose beneath her hand
The fairest Knight on Scottish mould
  Her brother, Ethert Brand!

Merry it is in good Greenwood,
  When the mavis and merle are singing,
But merrier were they in Dunfermline grey,
  When all the bells were ringing.
                          Sir Walter Scott

THE ERL-KING

Oʜ! who rides by night thro' the woodland so wild?
It is the fond father embracing his child;
And close the boy nestles within his loved arm,
To hold himself fast and to keep himself warm.

"O Father, see yonder! see yonder!" he says:
"My boy, upon what dost thou fearfully gaze?" —
"Oh! 't is the Erl-King with his crown and his
        shroud," —
"No, my Son, it is but a dark wreath of the cloud."

THE ERL-KING SPEAKS

"Oh! come and go with me, thou loveliest child;
By many a gay sport shall thy time be beguiled;
My mother keeps for thee full many a fair toy,
And many a fine flower shall she pluck for my boy."

"O Father, my Father! and did you not hear
The Erl-King whisper so low in my ear?" —
"Be still, my heart's darling — my child, be at
        ease;
It was but the wild blast as it sung thro' the
        trees."

THE ERL-KING SPEAKS AGAIN

"Oh! wilt thou go with me, thou loveliest boy?
My daughter shall tend thee with care and with joy;

She shall bear thee so lightly thro' wet and thro' wild,
And press thee and kiss thee and sing to my child."

"O Father, my Father, and saw you not plain,
The Erl-King's pale daughter glide past thro' the
    rain?" —
"Oh, yes, my loved treasure, I knew it full soon:
It was the grey willow that danced to the moon."

THE ERL-KING SPEAKS AGAIN

"Oh! come and go with me, no longer delay,
Or else, silly child, I will drag thee away." —

"O Father! O Father! now, now keep your hold,
The Erl-King has seized me — his grasp is so
    cold!"

Sore trembled the father; he spurred thro' the
    wild,
Clasping close to his bosom his shuddering child;
He reaches his dwelling in doubt and in dread,
But, clasped to his bosom, the infant was *dead!*
               Sir Walter Scott, from Goethe

THE FAIRY THORN

AN ULSTER BALLAD

"GET up, our Anna dear, from the weary spinning-
    wheel;
  For your father 's on the hill, and your mother
    is asleep:

Come up above the crags, and we'll dance a high-
        land reel
    Around the Fairy Thorn on the steep."

At Anna Grace's door 't was thus the maidens
        cried,
    Three merry maidens fair in kirtles of the green;
And Anna laid the rock and the weary wheel aside,
    The fairest of the four, I ween.

They're glancing thro' the glimmer of the quiet
        eve,
    Away in milky wavings of neck and ankle bare;
The heavy-sliding stream in its sleepy song they
        leave,
    And the crags in the ghostly air:

And linking hand in hand, and singing as they go,
    The maids along the hill-side have ta'en their
        fearless way
Till they come to where the Rowan Trees in lonely
        beauty grow
    Beside the Fairy Hawthorn grey.

The Hawthorn stands between the ashes tall and
        slim,
    Like matron with her twin grand-daughters at
        her knee;
The Rowan berries cluster o'er her low head grey
        and dim,
    In ruddy kisses sweet to see.

The merry maidens four have ranged them in a
    row,
    Between each lovely couple a stately Rowan
       stem,
And away in mazes wavy like skimming birds
    they go,
    Oh, never carolled bird like them!

But solemn is the silence of the silvery haze
    That drinks away their voices in echoless repose,
And dreamily the evening has stilled the haunted
      braes,
    And dreamier the gloaming grows.

And sinking one by one, like lark-notes from the
    sky
    When the falcon's shadow saileth across the
      open shaw,
Are hushed the maidens' voices as cowering down
    they lie
    In the flutter of their sudden awe.

For, from the air above, and the grassy ground be-
    neath
    And from the Mountain Ashes and the old
      Whitethorn between,
A power of faint Enchantment doth through their
    beings breathe
    And they sink down together on the green.

They sink together silent, and stealing side to
    side,
    They fling their lovely arms o'er their drooping
        necks so fair,
Then vainly strive again their naked arms to hide,
    For their shrinking necks again are bare.

Thus clasped and prostrate all, with their heads
    together bowed,
    Soft o'er their bosoms beating — the only hu-
        man sound —
They hear the silky footsteps of the silent Fairy
    crowd,
    Like a river in the air, gliding round.

Nor scream can any raise, nor prayer can any say,
    But wild, wild the terror of the speechless
        three —
For they feel fair Anna Grace drawn silently away,
    By whom they dare not look to see.

They feel her tresses twine with their parting locks
    of gold,
    And the curls elastic falling, as her head with-
        draws;
They feel her sliding arms from their tranced arms
    unfold,
    But they dare not look to see the cause:

For heavy on their senses the faint Enchantment
lies;
Through all that night of anguish and peril-
ous amaze;
And neither fear nor wonder can ope their quivering eyes
Or their limbs from the cold ground raise.

Till out of Night the Earth has rolled her dewy
side,
With every haunted mountain and streamy
vale below;
When, as the mist dissolves in the yellow morning
tide,
The maidens' trance dissolveth so.

Then fly the ghastly three as swiftly as they may,
And tell their tale of sorrow to anxious friends
in vain —
They pined away and died within the year and
day,
And ne'er was Anna Grace seen again.

Samuel Ferguson

LA BELLE DAME SANS MERCI

AH, what can ail thee, wretched wight,
Alone and palely loitering?
The sedge is withered from the lake
And no birds sing.

Ah, what can ail thee, wretched wight,
  So haggard and so woe-begone?
The squirrel's granary is full,
  And the harvest 's done.

I see a lily on thy brow,
  With anguish moist and fever dew;
And on thy cheek a fading rose
  Fast withereth too.

"I met a lady in the meads,
  Full beautiful — a Faery's child;
Her hair was long, her foot was light,
  And her eyes were wild.

"I set her on my pacing steed,
  And nothing else saw all day long;
For sideways would she lean, and sing
  A Faery's song.

"I made a garland for her head,
  And bracelets too, and fragrant zone;
She looked at me as she did love,
  And made sweet moan.

"She found me roots of relish sweet,
  And honey wild, and manna dew;
And sure in language strange she said, —
  'I love thee true.'

"She took me to her Elfin grot,
  And there she gazed and sighed deep,
And there I shut her wild sad eyes —
  So kissed to sleep.

"And there we slumbered on the moss,
  And there I dreamed — Ah, woe betide!
The latest dream I ever dreamed
  On the cold hill-side.

"I saw pale Kings and Princes too,
  Pale warriors, death-pale were they all;
Who cried, 'La Belle Dame sans Merci
  Hath thee in thrall!'

"I saw their starved lips in the gloom
  With horrid warning gaped wide,
And I awoke, and found me here
  On the cold hill-side.

"And this is why I sojourn here,
  Alone and palely loitering,
Though the sedge is withered from the lake,
  And no birds sing."
                        John Keats

THOMAS THE RHYMER

True Thomas lay on Huntlie bank;
  A ferlie he spied wi his e'e;
And there he saw a lady bright,
  Come riding down by the Eildon Tree.

Her shirt was o the grass-green silk,
  Her mantle o the velvet fyne;
At ilka tett of her horse's mane,
  Hang fifty siller bells and nine

True Thomas he pull'd aff his cap,
  And louted low down to his knee;
"All hail, thou mighty Queen of Heaven!
  For thy peer on earth I never did see." —

"O no, O no, Thomas," she said,
  'That name does not belang to me;
I am but the Queen of fair elfland,
  That am hither come to visit thee."

"Harp and carp, Thomas," she said;
  " Harp and carp along wi me;
And if ye dare to kiss my lips,
  Sure of your bodie I will be." —

"Betide me weal, betide me woe,
  That weird shall never daunton me."—
Syne he has kissed her rosy lips,
  All underneath the Eildon Tree.

"Now, ye maun go wi me," she said;
  "True Thomas, ye maun go wi me,
And ye maun serve me seven years,
  Thro weal or woe as may chance to be."

She mounted on her milk-white steed,
  She's ta'en True Thomas up behind:
And aye, whene'er her bridle rung,
  The steed flew swifter than the wind.

O they rade on, and farther on, —
  The steed gaed swifter than the wind:
Until they reached a desart wide,
  And living land was left behind.

"Light down, light down, now, True Thomas,
  And lean your head upon my knee;
Abide and rest a little space,
  And I will show you ferlies three.

"O see ye not yon narrow road,
  So thick beset with thorns and briers?
That is the path of righteousness.
  Tho after it but few enquires.

"And see not ye that braid, braid road,
  That lies across the lily leven?
That is the path of wickedness,
  Tho some call it the road to heaven.

"And see not ye that bonny road,
  That winds about the fernie brae?
That is the road to fair Elfland,
  Where you and I this night maun gae.

"But, Thomas, ye maun hold your tongue,
  Whatever ye may hear or see;
For if you speak word in Elfyn land,
  Ye 'll ne'er get back to your ain countrie."

O they rade on, and farther on,
  And they waded thro rivers aboon the knee,
And they saw neither sun nor moon,
  But they heard the roaring of the sea.

It was mirk, mirk night, and there was nae stern-
      light,
  And they waded thro red blude to the knee;
For a' the blude that 's shed on earth
  Rins thro the springs o that countrie.

Syne they came on to a garden green,
  And she pu'd an apple frae a tree:
"Take this for thy wages, True Thomas;
  It will give the tongue that can never lie."

"My tongue is mine ain," True Thomas said,
  "A gudely gift ye wad gie to me!
I neither dought to buy nor sell,
  At fair or tryst where I may be.

"I dought neither speak to prince or peer,
  Nor ask of grace from fair ladye."
"Now hold thy peace!" the lady said,
  "For as I say so must it be."

He has gotten a coat of the even cloth,
And a pair of shoes of velvet green;
And till seven years were gane and past,
True Thomas on earth was never seen.

THE KELPIE OF CORRIEVRECKAN

PART I

HE mounted his steed of the water clear,
And sat on his saddle of sea-weed sere;
He held his bridle of strings of pearl,
Dug out of the depths where the sea-snakes curl.

He put on his vest of the whirlpool froth,
Soft and dainty as velvet cloth,
And donned his mantle of sand so white,
And grasped his sword of the coral bright.

And away he galloped, a horseman free,
Spurring his steed through the stormy sea,
Clearing the billows with bound and leap —
Away, away, o'er the foaming deep!

By Scarba's rock, by Lunga's shore,
By Garveloch isles where the breakers roar,
With his horse's hoofs he dashed the spray,
And on to Loch Buy, away, away!

On to Loch Buy all day he rode,
And reached the shore as sunset glowed,
And stopped to hear the sounds of joy
That rose from the hills and glens of Moy.

The morrow was May, and on the green
They'd lit the fire of Beltan E'en,
And danced around, and piled it high
With peat and heather and pine-logs dry.

A piper played a lightsome reel,
And timed the dance with toe and heel;
While wives looked on, as lad and lass
Trod it merrily o'er the grass.

And Jessie (fickle and fair was she)
Sat with Evan beneath a tree,
And smiled with mingled love and pride,
And half agreed to be his bride.

The Kelpie galloped o'er the green —
He seemed a Knight of noble mien,
And old and young stood up to see,
And wondered who the Knight could be.

His flowing locks were auburn bright,
His cheeks were ruddy, his eyes flashed light;
And as he sprang from his good grey steed,
He looked a gallant youth indeed.

And Jessie's fickle heart beat high,
As she caught the stranger's glancing eye:
And when he smiled, "Ah, well," thought she,
"I wish this Knight came courting me!"

He took two steps towards her seat —
"Wilt thou be mine, O Maiden sweet?"
He took her lily-white hand, and sighed,
"Maiden, Maiden, be my bride!"

And Jessie blushed, and whispered soft —
"Meet me to-night when the moon's aloft;
I've dreamed, fair Knight, long time of thee —
I thought thou camest courting me."

PART II

WHEN the moon her yellow horn displayed,
Alone to the trysting went the maid;
When all the stars were shining bright,
Alone to the trysting went the Knight.

"I have loved thee long, I have loved thee well,
Maiden, oh more than words can tell!
Maiden, thine eyes like diamonds shine;
Maiden, Maiden, be thou mine!"

"Fair Sir, thy suit I'll ne'er deny —
Though poor my lot, my hopes are high;
I scorn a lover of low degree —
None but a Knight shall marry me."

He took her by the hand so white,
And gave her a ring of the gold so bright;
"Maiden, whose eyes like diamonds shine —
Maiden, Maiden, now thou 'rt mine!"

He lifted her up on his steed of grey,
And they rode till morning away, away —
Over the mountain and over the moor,
And over the rocks, to the dark sea-shore.

"We have ridden East, we have ridden West —
I'm weary, fair Knight, and I fain would rest,
Say, is thy dwelling beyond the sea?
Hast thou a good ship waiting for me?"

"I have no dwelling beyond the sea,
I have no good ship waiting for thee;
Thou shalt sleep with me on a couch of foam,
And the depths of the ocean shall be thy home."

The grey steed plunged in the billows clear,
And the maiden's shrieks were sad to hear.
"Maiden, whose eyes like diamonds shine —
Maiden, Maiden, now thou 'rt mine!"

Loud the cold sea-blast did blow,
As they sank 'mid the angry waves below —
Down to the rocks where the serpents creep,
Twice five hundred fathoms deep.

At morn a fisherman, sailing by,
Saw her pale corse floating high;
He knew the maid by her yellow hair
And her lily skin so soft and fair.

Under a rock on Scarba's shore,
Where the wild winds sigh and the breakers
    roar,
They dug her a grave by the water clear,
Among the sea-weed salt and seer.

And every year at Beltan E'en,
The Kelpie gallops across the green,
On a steed as fleet as the wintry wind,
With Jessie's mournful ghost behind.

I warn you, maids, whoever you be,
Beware of pride and vanity;
And ere on change of love you reckon,
Beware the Kelpie of Corrievreckan.

                Charles Mackay

KILMENY

BONNY KILMENY gaed up the glen;
But it wasna to meet Duneira's men,
Nor the rosy monk of the isle to see,
For Kilmeny was pure as pure could be.
It was only to hear the yorlin sing,
And pu' the cress-flower round the spring;

The scarlet hypp and the hindberrye,
And the nut that hang frae the hazel tree;
For Kilmeny was pure as pure could be.
But lang may her minny look o'er the wa',
And lang may she seek i' the green-wood shaw;
Lang the laird of Duneira blame,
And lang, lang greet or Kilmeny come hame!

When many a day had come and fled,
When grief grew calm, and hope was dead,
When mess for Kilmeny's soul had been sung,
When the bedes-man had prayed, and the dead
        bell rung,
Late, late in a gloamin when all was still,
When the fringe was red on the westlin hill,
The wood was sere, the moon i' the wane,
The reek o' the cot hung over the plain,
Like a little wee cloud in the world its lane;
When the ingle lowed with a eiry leme,
Late, late in the gloamin Kilmeny came hame!

"Kilmeny, Kilmeny, where have you been?
Lang hae we sought baith holt and den;
By linn, by ford, and green-wood tree,
Yet you are halesome and fair to see.
Where gat you that joup o' the lily scheen?
That bonny snood of the birk sae green?
And these roses, the fairest that ever were seen?
Kilmeny, Kilmeny, where have you been?"

Kilmeny looked up with a lovely grace,
But nae smile was seen on Kilmeny's face;
As still was her look, and as still was her e'e,
As the stillness that lay on the emerant lea,
Or the mist that sleeps on a waveless sea.
For Kilmeny had been she knew not where,
And Kilmeny had seen what she could not de-
    clare;
Kilmeny had been where the cock never crew,
Where the rain never fell, and the wind never blew;
But it seemed as the harp of the sky had rung,
And the airs of heaven played round her tongue,
When she spake of the lovely forms she had seen,
And a land where sin had never been;
A land of love, and a land of light,
Withouten sun, or moon, or night;
Where the river swa'd a living stream,
And the light a pure celestial beam:
The land of vision it would seem,
A still, an everlasting dream.

In yon green-wood there is a waik,
And in that waik there is a wene,
    And in that wene there is a maik
That neither has flesh, blood, nor bane;
And down in yon green-wood he walks his lane.

In that green wene Kilmeny lay,
Her bosom happed wi' the flowerets gay;

But the air was soft and the silence deep,
And bonny Kilmeny fell sound asleep.
She kend nae mair, nor opened her e'e,
Till waked by the hymns of a far countrye.

She 'wakened on a couch of the silk sae slim,
All striped wi' the bars of the rainbow's rim;
And lovely beings round were rife,
Who erst had travelled mortal life;
And aye they smiled, and 'gan to speer,
"What spirit has brought this mortal here!"

"Lang have I journeyed the world wide,"
A meek and reverend Fere replied;
"Baith night and day I have watched the fair,
Eident a thousand years and mair.
Yes, I have watched o'er ilk degree,
Wherever blooms femenitye;
But sinless virgin, free of stain
In mind and body, fand I nane.
Never, since the banquet of time,
Found I a virgin in her prime,
Till late this bonny maiden I saw
As spotless as the morning snaw:
Full twenty years she has lived as free
As the spirits that sojourn in this countrye:
I have brought her away frae the snares of
        men,
That sin or death she never may ken." —

They clasped her waist and her hands sae fair,
They kissed her cheek, and they kemed her hair,
And round came many a blooming Fere,
Saying, "Bonny Kilmeny, ye're welcome here!
Women are freed of the littand scorn:
O, blessed be the day Kilmeny was born!
Now shall the land of the spirits see,
Now shall it ken what a woman may be!
Many a lang year in sorrow and pain,
Many a lang year through the world we've gane,
Commissioned to watch fair womankind,
For it's they who nurice the immortal mind.
We have watched their steps as the dawning shone,
And deep in the green-wood walks alone;
By lily bower and silken bed,
The viewless tears have o'er them shed;
Have soothed their ardent minds to sleep,
Or left the couch of love to weep.
We have seen! we have seen! but the time must
     come,
And the Angels will weep at the day of doom!

"O, would the fairest of mortal kind
Aye keep the holy truths in mind,
That kindred spirits their motions see,
Who watch their ways with anxious e'e,
And grieve for the guilt of humanitye!
O, sweet to Heaven the maiden's prayer,
And the sigh that heaves a bosom sae fair!

And dear to Heaven the words of truth,
And the praise of virtue frae beauty's mouth!
And dear to the viewless forms of air,
The minds that kythe as the body fair!

"O, bonny Kilmeny! free frae stain,
If ever you seek the world again,
That world of sin, of sorrow, and fear,
O, tell of the joys that are waiting here;
And tell of the signs you shall shortly see;
Of the times that are now, and the times that
    shall be."

They lifted Kilmeny, they led her away,
And she walked in the light of a sunless day:
The sky was a dome of crystal bright,
The fountain of vision, and fountain of light:
The emerald fields were of dazzling glow,
And the flowers of everlasting blow.
Then deep in the stream her body they laid,
That her youth and beauty never might fade;
And they smiled on Heaven, when they saw her lie
In the stream of life that wandered bye.
And she heard a song, she heard it sung,
She kend not where; but sae sweetly it rung,
It fell on her ear like a dream of the morn —
"O, blest be the day Kilmeny was born!
Now shall the land of the spirits see,
Now shall it ken what a woman may be!

The sun that shines on the world sae bright,
A borrowed gleid frae the fountain of light;
And the moon that sleeks the sky sae dun,
Like a gouden bow, or a beamless sun,
Shall wear away, and be seen nae mair,
And the Angels shall miss them travelling the
     air.
But lang, lang after baith night and day,
When the sun and the world have elyed away;
When the sinner has gane to his waesome doom,
Kilmeny shall smile in eternal bloom!"

   They bore her away, she wist not how,
For she felt not arm nor rest below;
But so swift they wained her through the light,
'T was like the motion of sound or sight;
They seemed to split the gales of air,
And yet nor gale nor breeze was there.
Unnumbered groves below them grew,
They came, they past, and backward flew,
Like floods of blossoms gliding on,
In moment seen, in moment gone.
O, never vales to mortal view
Appeared like those o'er which they flew!
That land to human spirits given,
The lowermost vales of the storied Heaven;
From thence they can view the world below,
And Heaven's blue gates with sapphires glow,
More glory yet unmeet to know.

They bore her far to a mountain green,
To see what mortal never had seen;
And they seated her high on a purple sward,
And bade her heed what she saw and heard,
And note the changes the spirits wrought,
For now she lived in the Land of Thought.
She looked, and she saw nor sun nor skies,
But a crystal dome of a thousand dies:
She looked, and she saw nae land aright,
But an endless whirl of glory and light:
And radiant beings went and came
Far swifter than wind, or the linked flame.
She hid her e'en frae the dazzling view;
She looked again, and the scene was new.

But to sing the sights Kilmeny saw,
So far surpassing nature's law,
The singer's voice wad sink away,
And the string of his harp wad cease to play.
But she saw till the sorrows of man were bye,
And all was love and harmony;
Till the stars of Heaven fell calmly away,
Like the flakes of snaw on a winter day.

Then Kilmeny begged again to see
The friends she had left in her own countrye,
To tell of the place where she had been,
And the glories that lay in the land unseen;

To warn the living maidens fair,
The loved of Heaven, the spirits' care,
That all whose minds unmeled remain
Shall bloom in beauty when time is gane.

With distant music, soft and deep,
They lulled Kilmeny sound asleep;
And when she awakened, she lay her lane,
All happed with flowers in the green-wood wene.
When seven lang years had come and fled;
When grief was calm, and hope was dead;
When scarce was remembered Kilmeny's name,
Late, late in a gloamin Kilmeny came hame!
And O, her beauty was fair to see,
But still and steadfast was her e'e!
Such beauty bard may never declare,
For there was no pride nor passion there;
And the soft desire of maiden's e'en
In that mild face could never be seen.
Her seymar was the lily flower,
And her cheek the moss-rose in the shower;
And her voice like the distant melodye,
That floats along the twilight sea.
But she loved to raike the lanely glen,
And keeped afar frae the haunts of men;
Her holy hymns unheard to sing,
To suck the flowers, and drink the spring.
But wherever her peaceful form appeared,
The wild beasts of the hill were cheered;

The wolf played blythely round the field,
The lordly byson lowed and kneeled;
The dun deer wooed with manner bland,
And cowered aneath her lily hand.
And when at even the woodlands rung,
When hymns of other worlds she sung,
In ecstasy of sweet devotion,
O, then the glen was all in motion!
The wild beasts of the forest came,
Broke from their bughts and faulds the tame,
And goved around, charmed and amazed;
Even the dull cattle crooned and gazed,
And murmured and looked with anxious pain
For something the mystery to explain.

The buzzard came with the throstle-cock;
The corby left her houf in the rock;
The blackbird alang wi' the eagle flew;
The hind came tripping o'er the dew;
The wolf and the kid their raike began,
And the tod, and the lamb, and the leveret ran;
The hawk and the hern attour them hung,
And the merl and the mavis forhooyed their
        young;
And all in a peaceful ring were hurled:
It was like an eve in a sinless world!

When a month and a day had come and gane,
Kilmeny sought the green-wood wene;

There laid her down on the leaves sae green,
And Kilmeny on earth was never mair seen.
But, O, the words that fell from her mouth,
Were words of wonder and words of truth!
But all the land were in fear and dread,
For they kendna whether she was living or dead.
It wasna her hame, and she couldna remain;
She left this world of sorrow and pain,
And returned to the Land of Thought again.

The Ettrick Shepherd. (Condensed)

LAYS O' WONDER

THE WEE WEE MAN

As I was walking all alane,
  Between a water and a wa',
And there I spied a wee wee man,
  And he was the least that e'er I saw.

His legs were scarce a shathmont's length,
  And thick and thimber was his thie;
Between his brows there was a span,
  And between his shoulders there was three.

He took up a meikle stane,
  And he flang 't as far as I could see;
Though I had been a Wallace wight,
  I couldna liften 't to my knee.

"O, wee wee man, but thou art strang!
  O tell me where thy dwelling be?"
"My dwelling's down by yon bonny bower,
  O will you go with me and see?"

On we lap, and awa' we rade,
  Till we came to yon bonny green;
We lighted down to bait our horse,
  And out there came a lady fine.

Four-and-twenty at her back,
  And they were a' clad out in green;
Though the King of Scotland had been there,
  The warst o' them might hae been his queen.

On we lap, and awa' we rade,
  Till we came to yon bonny ha',
Where the roof was o' the beaten gowd,
  And the floor was o' the crystal a'.

When we came to the stair foot,
  Ladies were dancing jimp and sma';
But in the twinkling o' an ee,
  My wee wee man was clean awa'.

THE EARL OF MAR'S DAUGHTER

Iᴛ was intill a pleasant time,
   Upon a simmer's day,
The noble Earl of Mar's daughter
   Went forth to sport and play.

As thus she did amuse hersell,
   Below a green aik tree,
There she saw a sprightly doo
   Set on a tower sae hie.

"O Cow-me-doo, my love sae true,
   If ye'll come down to me,
Ye'se hae a cage o guid red gowd
   Instead o simple tree:

"I'll put gowd hingers roun your cage,
   And siller roun your wa;
I'll gar ye shine as fair a bird
   As ony o them a'."

But she hadnae these words well spoke,
   Nor yet these words well said,
Till Cow-me-doo flew frae the tower
   And lighted on her head.

Then she has brought this pretty bird
　　Hame to her bowers and ha,
And made him shine as fair a bird
　　As ony o them a'.

When day was gane, and night was come,
　　About the evening tide,
This lady spied a sprightly youth
　　Stand straight up by her side.

"From whence came ye, young man?" she said;
　　"That does surprise me sair;
My door was bolted right secure,
　　What way hae ye come here?"

"O had your tongue, ye lady fair,
　　Lat a' your folly be;
Mind ye not on your turtle-doo
　　Last day ye brought wi thee?"

"O tell me mair, young man," she said,
　　"This does surprise me now;
What country hae ye come frae?
　　What pedigree are you?"

"My mither lives on foreign isles,
　　She has nae mair but me;
She is a queen o wealth and state,
　　And birth and high degree.

"Likewise well skilld in magic spells,
  As ye may plainly see,
And she transformd me to yon shape,
  To charm such maids as thee.

"I am a doo the live-lang day,
  A sprightly youth at night;
This aye gars me appear mair fair
  In a fair maiden's sight.

"And it was but this verra day
  That I came ower the sea;
Your lovely face did me enchant;
  I'll live and dee wi thee."

"O Cow-me-doo, my luve sae true,
  Nae mair frae me ye'se gae;"
"That's never my intent, my luve,
  As ye said, it shall be sae."

"O Cow-me-doo, my luve sae true,
  It's time for us to wed;"
"Wi a' my heart, my dear marrow,
  It's be as ye hae said."

PART II

THEN he has staid in bower wi her
  For sax lang years and ane,
Till sax young sons to him she bare,
  And the seventh she's brought hame.

But aye as ever a child was born
    He carried them away,
And brought them to his mither's care,
    As fast as he coud fly.

Thus he has staid in bower wi her
    For twenty years and three;
There came a lord o high renown
    To court this fair ladie.

But still his proffer she refused,
    And a' his presents too;
Says, "I'm content to live alane
    Wi my bird, Cow-me-doo."

Her father sware a solemn oath
    Amang the nobles all,
"The morn, or ere I eat or drink,
    This bird I will gar kill."

The bird was sitting in his cage,
    And heard what they did say;
And when he found they were dismist,
    Says, "Wae's me for this day!

"Before that I do langer stay,
    And thus to be forlorn,
I'll gang unto my mither's bower,
    Where I was bred and born."

Then Cow-me-doo took flight and flew
    Beyond the raging sea,
And lighted near his mither's castle,
    On a tower o gowd sae hie.

As his mither was wauking out,
    To see what she coud see,
And there she saw her little son,
    Set on the tower sae hie.

"Get dancers here to dance," she said,
    "And minstrells for to play;
For here's my young son, Florentine,
    Come here wi me to stay."

"Get nae dancers to dance, mither,
    Nor minstrells for to play,
For the mither o my seven sons,
    The morn's her wedding-day."

"O tell me, tell me, Florentine,
    Tell me, and tell me true,
Tell me this day without a flaw,
    What I will do for you."

"Instead of dancers to dance, mither,
    Or minstrells for to play,
Turn four-and-twenty wall-wight men
    Like storks in feathers gray;

"My seven sons in seven swans,
   Aboon their heads to flee;
And I mysell a gay gos-hawk,
   A bird o high degree."

Then sichin said the queen hersell,
   "That thing's too high for me;"
But she applied to an auld woman,
   Who had mair skill than she.

Instead o dancers to dance a dance,
   Or minstrells for to play,
Four-and-twenty wall-wight men
   Turnd birds o feathers gray;

Her seven sons in seven swans,
   Aboon their heads to flee;
And he himsell a gay gos-hawk,
   A bird o high degree.

This flock o birds took flight and flew
   Beyond the raging sea,
And landed near the Earl Mar's castle,
   Took shelter in every tree.

They were a flock o pretty birds,
   Right comely to be seen;
The people viewd them wi surprise,
   As they dancd on the green.

These birds ascended frae the tree
  And lighted on the ha,
And at the last wi force did flee
  Amang the nobles a'.

The storks there seized some o the men,
  They coud neither fight nor flee;
The swans they bound the bride's best man
  Below a green aik tree.

They lighted next on maidens fair,
  Then on the bride's own head,
And wi the twinkling o an ee
  The bride and them were fled.

There's ancient men at weddings been
  For sixty years or more,
But sic a curious wedding-day
  They never saw before.

For naething coud the companie do,
  Nor naething coud they say
But they saw a flock o pretty birds
  That took their bride away.

When that Earl Mar he came to know
  Where his dochter did stay,
He signd a bond o' unity,
  And visits now they pay.

KEMP OWYNE

HER mother died when she was young,
  Which gave her cause to make great moan;
Her father married the warst woman
  That ever lived in Christendom.

She served her with foot and hand,
  In every thing that she could dee,
Till once, in an unlucky time,
  She threw her in ower Craigy's sea.

Says, "Lie you there, dove Isabel,
  And all my sorrows lie with thee;
Till Kemp Owyne come ower the sea,
  And borrow you with kisses three,
Let all the warld do what they will,
  Oh borrowed shall you never be!"

Her breath grew strang, her hair grew lang,
  And twisted thrice about the tree,
And all the people, far and near,
  Thought that a savage beast was she.

These news did come to Kemp Owyne,
  Where he lived, far beyond the sea;
He hasted him to Craigy's sea,
  And on the savage beast lookd he.

Her breath was strang, her hair was lang,
  And twisted was about the tree,
And with a swing she came about:
  "Come to Craigy's sea, and kiss with me.

"Here is a royal belt," she cried,
  "That I have found in the green sea;
And while your body it is on,
  Drawn shall your blood never be;
But if you touch me, tail or fin,
  I vow my belt your death shall be."

He stepped in, gave her a kiss,
  The royal belt he brought him wi;
Her breath was strang, her hair was lang,
  And twisted twice about the tree,
And with a swing she came about:
  "Come to Craigy's sea, and kiss with me.

"Here is a royal ring," she said,
  "That I have found in the green sea;
And while your finger it is on,
  Drawn shall your blood never be;
But if you touch me, tail or fin,
  I swear my ring your death shall be."

He stepped in, gave her a kiss,
  The royal ring he brought him wi;

Her breath was strang, her hair was lang,
  And twisted ance about the tree,
And with a swing she came about:
  "Come to Craigy's sea, and kiss with me.

"Here is a royal brand," she said,
  "That I have found in the green sea;
And while your body it is on,
  Drawn shall your blood never be;
But if you touch me, tail or fin,
  I swear my brand your death shall be."

He stepped in, gave her a kiss,
  The royal brand he brought him wi;
Her breath was sweet, her hair grew short,
  And twisted nane about the tree,
And smilingly she came about,
  As fair a woman as fair could be.

THE LADY OF SHALOTT

PART I

On either side the river lie
Long fields of barley and of rye,
That clothe the wold and meet the sky;
And thro' the field the road runs by
  To many-towered Camelot;
And up and down the people go,

Gazing where the lilies blow
Round an island there below,
   The island of Shalott.

Willows whiten, aspens quiver,
Little breezes dusk and shiver
Thro' the wave that runs for ever
By the island in the river
   Flowing down to Camelot.
Four grey walls, and four grey towers,
Overlook a space of flowers,
And the silent isle imbowers
   The Lady of Shalott.

By the margin, willow-veiled,
Slide the heavy barges trailed
By slow horses; and unhailed
The shallop flitteth silken-sailed
   Skimming down to Camelot;
But who hath seen her wave her hand?
Or at the casement seen her stand?
Or is she known in all the land,
   The Lady of Shalott?

Only reapers, reaping early
In among the bearded barley,
Hear a song that echoes cheerly
From the river winding clearly,
   Down to towered Camelot;

And by the moon the reaper weary,
Piling sheaves in uplands airy,
Listening, whispers "'T is the Fairy
    Lady of Shalott."

PART II

THERE she weaves by night and day
A magic web with colours gay.
She has heard a whisper say,
A curse is on her if she stay
    To look down to Camelot.
She knows not what the curse may be,
And so she weaveth steadily,
And little other care hath she,
    The Lady of Shalott.

And moving thro' a mirror clear
That hangs before her all the year,
Shadows of the world appear.
There she sees the highway near
    Winding down to Camelot;
There the river eddy whirls,
And there the surly village-churls,
And the red cloaks of market-girls,
    Pass onward from Shalott.

Sometimes a troop of damsels glad,
An abbot on an ambling pad,
Sometimes a curly shepherd-lad,
Or long-haired page in crimson clad,

Goes by to towered Camelot;
And sometimes thro' the mirror blue
The Knights come riding two and two:
She hath no loyal Knight and true,
　The Lady of Shalott.

But in her web she still delights
To weave the mirror's magic sights,
For often thro' the silent nights
A funeral, with plumes and lights
　And music, went to Camelot;
Or when the moon was overhead,
Came two young lovers lately wed:
"I am half sick of shadows," said
　The Lady of Shalott.

PART III

A BOW-SHOT from her bower-eaves,
He rode between the barley-sheaves,
The sun came dazzling thro' the leaves,
And flamed upon the brazen greaves
　Of bold Sir Lancelot.
A Red-cross Knight for ever kneeled
To a lady in his shield,
That sparkled on the yellow field,
　Beside remote Shalott.

The gemmy bridle glittered free,
Like to some branch of stars we see

Hung in the golden Galaxy.
The bridle-bells rang merrily
    As he rode down to Camelot:
And from his blazoned baldric slung
A mighty silver bugle hung,
And as he rode his armour rung,
    Beside remote Shalott.

All in the blue unclouded weather
Thick-jewelled shone the saddle-leather,
The helmet and the helmet-feather
Burned like one burning flame together,
    As he rode down to Camelot;
As often thro' the purple night,
Below the starry clusters bright,
Some bearded meteor, trailing light,
    Moves over still Shalott.

His broad clear brow in sunlight glowed;
On burnished hooves his war-horse trode;
From underneath his helmet flowed
His coal-black curls as on he rode,
    As he rode down to Camelot.
From the bank and from the river
He flashed into the crystal mirror,
"Tirra lirra," by the river
    Sang Sir Lancelot.

She left the web, she left the loom,
She made three paces thro' the room,

She saw the water-lily bloom,
She saw the helmet and the plume,
  She looked down to Camelot.
Out flew the web and floated wide;
The mirror cracked from side to side;
"The curse is come upon me," cried
  The Lady of Shalott.

PART IV

In the stormy east-wind straining,
The pale yellow woods were waning,
The broad stream in his banks complaining,
Heavily the low sky raining
  Over towered Camelot;
Down she came and found a boat
Beneath a willow left afloat,
And round about the prow she wrote
  The Lady of Shalott.

And down the river's dim expanse
Like some bold seër in a trance,
Seeing all his own mischance —
With a glassy countenance
  Did she look to Camelot.
And at the closing of the day
She loosed the chain, and down she lay;
The broad stream bore her far away,
  The Lady of Shalott.

Lying, robed in snowy white
That loosely flew to left and right —
The leaves upon her falling light —
Thro' the noises of the night
   She floated down to Camelot;
And as the boat-head wound along
The willowy hills and fields among,
They heard her singing her last song,
   The Lady of Shalott.

Heard a carol, mournful, holy,
Chanted loudly, chanted lowly,
Till her blood was frozen slowly,
And her eyes were darkened wholly,
   Turned to towered Camelot.
For ere she reached upon the tide
The first house by the water-side,
Singing in her song she died,
   The Lady of Shalott.

Under tower and balcony,
By garden-wall and gallery,
A gleaming shape she floated by,
Dead-pale between the houses high,
   Silent into Camelot.
Out upon the wharfs they came,
Knight and burgher, lord and dame,
And round the prow they read her name,
   The Lady of Shalott.

Who is this? and what is here?
And in the lighted palace near
Died the sound of royal cheer;
And they crossed themselves for fear,
    All the Knights at Camelot:
But Lancelot mused a little space;
He said, "She has a lovely face;
God in his mercy lend her grace,
    The Lady of Shalott."

Alfred, Lord Tennyson

THE SINGING LEAVES

I

"WHAT fairings will ye that I bring?"
    Said the King to his daughters three;
"For I to Vanity Fair am boun',
    Now say what shall they be?"

Then up and spake the eldest daughter,
    That lady tall and grand:
"Oh, bring me pearls and diamonds great,
    And gold rings for my hand."

Thereafter spake the second daughter,
    That was both white and red:
"For me bring silks that will stand alone,
    And a gold comb for my head."

Then came the turn of the least daughter,
  That was whiter than thistle-down,
And among the gold of her blithesome hair
  Dim shone the golden crown.

"There came a bird this morning,
  And sang 'neath my bower eaves,
Till I dreamed, as his music made me,
  'Ask thou for the Singing Leaves.'"

Then the brow of the King swelled crimson
  With a flush of angry scorn:
"Well have ye spoken, my two eldest,
  And chosen as ye were born;

"But she, like a thing of peasant race,
  That is happy binding the sheaves;"
Then he saw her dead mother in her face,
  And said, "Thou shalt have thy leaves."

II

HE mounted and rode three days and nights
  Till he came to Vanity Fair,
And 't was easy to buy the gems and the silk,
  But no Singing Leaves were there.

Then deep in the Greenwood rode he,
  And asked of every tree,
"Oh, if you have ever a Singing Leaf,
  I pray you give it me!"

But the trees all kept their counsel,
   And never a word said they,
Only there sighed from the pine-tops
   A music of seas far away.

Only the pattering aspen
   Made a sound of growing rain,
That fell ever faster and faster,
   Then faltered to silence again.

"Oh, where shall I find a little foot-page
   That would win both hose and shoon,
And will bring to me the Singing Leaves
   If they grow under the moon?"

Then lightly turned him Walter the page,
   By the stirrup as he ran:
"Now pledge you me the truesome word
   Of a King and gentleman,

"That you will give me the first, first thing
   You meet at your castle-gate,
And the Princess shall get the Singing Leaves,
   Or mine be a traitor's fate."

The King's head dropt upon his breast
   A moment, as it might be;
'T will be my dog, he thought, and said,
   "My faith I plight to thee."

Then Walter took from next his heart
  A packet small and thin,
"Now give you this to the Princess Anne,
  The Singing Leaves are therein."

III

As the King rode in at his castle-gate,
  A maiden to meet him ran,
And "Welcome, Father!" she laughed and cried
  Together, the Princess Anne.

"Lo, here the Singing Leaves," quoth he,
  "And woe, but they cost me dear!"
She took the packet, and the smile
  Deepened down beneath the tear.

It deepened down till it reached her heart,
  And then gushed up again,
And lighted her tears as the sudden sun
  Transfigures the summer rain.

And the first Leaf, when it was opened,
  Sang: "I am Walter the page,
And the songs I sing 'neath thy window
  Are my only heritage."

And the second Leaf sang, "But in the land
  That is neither on earth nor sea,
My lute and I are lords of more
  Than thrice this kingdom's fee."

And the third Leaf sang, "Be mine! Be mine!"
 And ever it sang, "Be mine!"
Then sweeter it sang and ever sweeter,
 And said, "I am thine, thine, thine!"

At the first Leaf she grew pale enough,
 At the second she turned aside,
At the third, 't was as if a lily flushed
 With a rose's red heart's tide.

"Good counsel gave the bird," said she,
 "I have my hope thrice o'er,
For they sing to my very heart," she said,
 "And it sings to them evermore."

She brought to him her beauty and truth,
 But and broad earldoms three,
And he made her Queen cf the broader lands
 He held of his lute in fee.

       James Russell Lowell

THE LUCK OF EDENHALL

Of Edenhall, the youthful Lord
Bids sound the festal trumpet's call;
He rises at the banquet board,
And cries, 'mid the drunken revellers all:
"Now bring me the Luck of Edenhall!"

The butler hears the words with pain,
The house's oldest seneschal,
Takes slow from its silken cloth again
The drinking-glass of crystal tall;
  They call it the Luck of Edenhall.

Then said the Lord: "This glass to praise,
Fill with red wine from Portugal!"
The greybeard with trembling hand obeys;
A purple light shines over all,
It beams from the Luck of Edenhall.

Then speaks the Lord, and waves it light:
"This glass of flashing crystal tall
Gave to my sires the Fountain-Sprite;
  She wrote in it, *If this glass doth fall,*
Farewell then, O Luck of Edenhall!

"'T was right a goblet the Fate should be
Of the joyous race of Edenhall!
Deep draughts drink we right willingly
And willingly ring, with merry call,
Kling! klang! to the Luck of Edenhall!"

First rings it deep, and full, and mild,
Like to the song of a nightingale;
Then like the roar of a torrent wild;
Then mutters at last like the thunder's fall,
The glorious Luck of Edenhall.

"For its keeper takes a race of might,
The fragile goblet of crystal tall;
It has lasted longer than is right;
Kling! klang! — with a harder blow than all
Will I try the Luck of Edenhall!"

As the goblet ringing flies apart,
Suddenly cracks the vaulted hall;
And through the rift, the wild flames start;
The guests in dust are scattered all,
With the breaking Luck of Edenhall!

In storms the foe, with fire and sword;
He in the night had scaled the wall,
Slain by the sword lies the youthful Lord,
But holds in his hand the crystal tall,
The shattered Luck of Edenhall.

On the morrow the butler gropes alone,
The greybeard in the desert hall,
He seeks his Lord's burnt skeleton,
He seeks in the dismal ruin's fall
The shards of the Luck of Edenhall.

"The stone wall," saith he, "doth fall aside,
Down must the stately columns fall;
Glass is this earth's Luck and Pride;
In atoms shall fall this earthly ball
One day like the Luck of Edenhall!"

Henry Wadsworth Longfellow, from Uhland

MAY OF THE MORIL GLEN

PART I

I WILL tell you of ane wondrous tale,
   As ever was told by man,
Or ever was sung by minstrel meet
   Since this base world began: —

It is of ane May, and ane lovely May,
   That dwelt in the Moril Glen,
The fairest flower of mortal frame,
   But a devil amongst the men;

For nine of them sticket themselves for love,
   And ten leaped in the main,
And seven-and-thirty brake their hearts,
   And never loved women again.

But this bonnie May, she never knew
   A father's kindly claim;
She never was blessed in holy Church,
   Nor christened in holy name.

But there she lived an earthly flower
   Of beauty so supreme,
Some feared she was of the Mermaid's brood,
   Come out of the salt sea faeme.

Some said she was found in a Fairy Ring,
   And born of the Fairy Queen;
For there was a rainbow behind the moon
   That night she first was seen.

And no man could look on her face
   And eyne that beamed so clear
But felt a sting go through his heart,
   Far sharper than a spear.

So that around the Moril Glen
   Our brave young men did lie,
With limbs as lydder and as lithe
   As duddis hung out to dry.

And aye the tears ran down in streams
   O'er cheeks right woe-begone;
And aye they gasped, and they gratte,
   And thus made piteous moan: —

"Alack! that I had ever been born,
   Or dandelit on the knee;
Or rockit in ane cradle bed,
   Beneath a mother's e'e!

"For love is like the fiery flame
   That quivers through the rain,
And love is like the pang of death
   That splits the heart in twain.

"If I had loved earthly thing
    Of earthly blithesomeness,
I might have been beloved again,
    And bathed in earthly bliss.

"But I have loved ane freakish Fay
    Of frowardness and sin,
With heavenly beauty on the face,
    And heart of stone within!"

PART II

BUT word's gone East, and word's gone West,
    'Mong high and low degree,
While it went to the King upon the throne,
    And ane wrathful man was he.

"What!" said the King, "and shall we sit
    In sackcloth mourning sad,
While all mine lieges of the land
    For ane young quean run mad?

"Go, saddle me my milk-white steed,
    Of true Megaira brode;
I will go and see this wondrous dame,
    And prove her by the Rode.

"And if I find her Elfin Queen,
    Or thing of Fairy kind,
I will burn her into ashes small,
    And sift them on the wind."

The King hath chosen four-score Knights,
  All busked gallantlye,
And he is away to the Moril Glen,
  As fast as he can dree.

And when he came to the Moril Glen,
  Ae morning fair and clear,
This lovely May on horseback rode
  To hunt the fallow deer.

Her palfrey was of snowy hue,
  A pale unearthly thing,
That revelled over hill and dale
  Like bird upon the wing.

Her screen was like a net of gold,
  That dazzled as it flew;
Her mantle was of the rainbow's red,
  Her rail of its bonny blue.

A golden comb with diamonds bright,
  Her seemly virgin crown,
Shone like the new moon's lady-light
  O'er cloud of amber brown.

The lightning that shot from her eyne,
  Flickered like Elfin brand;
It was sharper nor the sharpest spear
  In all Northumberland.

The King he wheeled him round about,
  And calleth to his men,
"Yonder she comes, this wierdly Witch,
  This spirit of the glen!

"Come, rank your master up behind,
  This serpent to belay;
I'll let you hear me put her down,
  In grand polemic way."

Swift came the maid o'er strath and stron —
  Nae dantonit dame was she, —
Until the King her path withstood
  In might and majestye.

The virgin cast on him a look,
  With gay and graceful air,
As on something below her note,
  That ought not to have been there.

The King, whose belt was like to burst,
  With speeches most divine,
Now felt ane throbbing of the heart,
  And quaking of the spine.

And aye he gasped for his breath,
  And gaped in dire dismay,
And waved his arm, and smote his breast;
  But word he could not say.

The spankie grewis they scoured the dale,
  The dun deer to restrain;
The virgin gave her steed the rein,
  And followed, might and main.

"Go bring her back," the King he cried;
  "This reifery must not be.
Though you should bind her hands and feet,
  Go, bring her back to me."

The deer she flew, the garf and grew
  They followed hard behind;
The milk-white palfrey brushed the dew
  Far fleeter nor the wind.

But woe betide the Lords and Knights,
  That taiglit in the dell!
For though with whip and spur they plied,
  Full far behind they fell.

They looked out o'er their left shoulders,
  To see what they might see,
And there the King, in fit of love,
  Lay spurring on the lea.

And, aye, he battered with his feet,
  And rowted with despair,
And pulled the grass up by the roots,
  And flung it on the air!

"What ails, what ails my royal Liege?
  Such grief I do deplore."
"Oh, I'm bewitched," the King replied,
  "And gone forevermore!

"Go, bring her back! — go, bring her back! —
  Go, bring her back to me!
For I must either die of love,
  Or own that dear Ladye!"

The deer was slain; the royal train
  Then closed the virgin round,
And then her fair and lily hands
  Behind her back were bound.

But who should bind her winsome feet? —
  That bred such strife and pain,
That sixteen brave and belted Knights
  Lay gasping on the plain.

And when she came before the King,
  Ane ireful carle was he;
Saith he, "Dame, you must be my love,
  Or burn beneath ane tree."

"No, I can ne'er be love to thee,
  Nor any lord thou hast;
For you are married men each one,
  And I a maiden chaste.

"But here I promise, and I vow
  By Scotland's King and Crown,
Who first a widower shall prove,
  Shall claim me as his own."

The King hath mounted his milk-white steed, —
  One word he said not more, —
And he is away from the Moril Glen,
  As ne'er rode King before.

And every Lord and every Knight
  Made off his several way,
All galloping as they had been mad,
  Withoutten stop or stay.

But there was never such dole and pain
  In any land befel;
For there is wickedness in man,
  That grieveth me to tell.

There was one eye, and one alone,
  Beheld the deeds were done;
But the lovely Queen of Fair Scotland
  Ne'er saw the morning sun.

And seventy-seven wedded dames,
  As fair as e'er were born,
The very pride of all the land,
  Were dead before the morn.

PART III

AND the bonny May of the Moril Glen
  Is weeping in despair,
For she saw the hills of fair Scotland,
  Could be her home nae mair.

Then there were chariots came o'er night,
  As silent and as soon
As shadow of ane little cloud
  In the wan light of the moon.

Some said they came out of the rock,
  And some out of the sea;
And some said they were sent from Hell
  To bring that fair Ladye.

The fairest flower of mortal frame
  Passed from the Moril Glen;
And ne'er may such a deadly eye
  Shine amongst Christian men!

In seven chariots, gilded bright,
  The train went o'er the fell,
All wrapt within ane shower of hail;
  Whither no man could tell.

But there was a Ship in the Firth of Forth,
  The like ne'er sailed the faeme,
For no man of her country knew,
  Her colours, or her name.

Her mast was made of beaten gold,
  Her sails of the silken twine,
And a thousand pennons streamed behind,
  And trembled o'er the brine.

As she lay mirrored in the main,
  It was a comely view,
So many rainbows round her played
  With every breeze that blew.

And the hailstone shroud it rattled loud,
  Right over ford and fen,
And swathed the flower of the Moril Glen
  From eyes of sinful men.

And the hailstone shroud it wheeled and rowed,
  As wan as death unshriven,
Like dead cloth of ane Angel grim,
  Or winding sheet of Heaven.

It was a fearsome sight to see
  Toil through the morning grey,
And whenever it reached the comely Ship,
  She set sail and away.

She set her sail before the gale,
  As it began to sing,
And she heaved and rocked down the tide,
  Unlike an earthly thing.

The dolphins fled out of her way
   Into the creeks of Fife,
And the blackguard seals, they yowlit for dread,
   And swam for death and life.

But aye the Ship, the bonny Ship
   Out o'er the green wave flew,
Swift as the solan on the wing,
   Or terrified sea-mew.

No billow breasted on her prow,
   Nor levelled on the lee;
She seemed to sail upon the air,
   And never touch the sea.

And away, and away went the bonny Ship,
   Which man never more did see;
But whether she went to Heaven or Hell,
   Was ne'er made known to me.
               The Ettrick Shepherd. (Condensed)

THE LAIDLEY WORM O' SPINDLESTON-HEUGHS

PART I

The King is gone from Bambrough Castle,
   Long may the Princess mourn;
Long may she stand on the Castle wall,
   Looking for his return.

She has knotted the keys upon a string,
  And with her she has them taen,
She has cast them o'er her left shoulder,
  And to the gate she is gane.

She tripped out, she tripped in,
  She tript into the yard;
But it was more for the King's sake,
  Than for the Queen's regard.

It fell out on a day, the King
  Brought the Queen with him home;
And all the Lords in our country,
  To welcome them did come.

"Oh welcome, Father!" the Lady cries,
  " Unto your halls and bowers;
And so are you, my Stepmother,
  For all that is here is yours."

A Lord said, wondering while she spake,
  "This Princess of the North
Surpasses all of female kind
  In beauty and in worth."

The envious Queen replied, "At least,
  You might have excepted me:
In a few hours I will her bring
  Down to a low degree.

"I will her liken to a Laidley Worm,
   That warps about the stone,
And not till Childy Wynd comes back,
   Shall she again be won."

PART II

THE Princess stood at the bower-door,
   Laughing, who could her blame?
But e'er the next day's sun went down,
   A long Worm she became.

For seven miles East, and seven miles West,
   And seven miles North, and South,
No blade of grass or corn could grow,
   So venomous was her mouth.

The milk of seven stately cows —
   It was costly her to keep —
Was brought her daily, which she drank
   Before she went to sleep.

At this day may be seen the cave
   Which held her folded up,
And the stone trough — the very same —
   Out of which she did sup.

Word went East, and word went West,
   And word is gone over the sea,
That a Laidley Worm in Spindleston-Heughs,
   Would ruin the North Countrie.

Word went East, and word went West,
  And over the sea did go;
The Child of Wynd got wit of it,
  Which filled his heart with woe.

He called straight his merry men all,
  They thirty were and three:
"I wish I were at Spindleston,
  This desperate Worm to see.

"We have no time now here to waste,
  Hence quickly let us sail:
My only sister Margaret
  Something, I fear, doth ail."

They built a ship without delay,
  With masts of the Rowan-Tree,
With fluttering sails of silk so fine,
  And set her on the sea.

They went aboard; the wind with speed,
  Blew them along the deep;
At length they spied an huge square tower
  On a rock high and steep.

The sea was smooth, the weather clear;
  When they approached nigher,
King Ida's Castle they well knew,
  And the banks of Bambroughshire.

PART III

THE Queen looked out at her bower-window,
  To see what she could see;
There she espied a gallant ship
  Sailing upon the sea.

When she beheld the silken sails,
  Full glancing in the sun,
To sink the ship she sent away
  Her Witch Wives every one.

Their spells were vain; the Hags returned
  To the Queen in sorrowful mood,
Crying, that Witches have no power
  Where there is Rowan-Tree wood.

Her last effort, she sent a boat,
  Which in the haven lay,
With armed men to board the ship,
  But they were driven away.

The Worm leapt up, the Worm leapt down,
  She plaited round the stane;
And aye, as the ship came to the land,
  She banged it off again.

The Child then ran out of her reach
  The ship on Budle-sand;
And jumping into the shallow sea,
  Securely got to land.

And now he drew his berry-brown sword,
  And laid it on her head;
And swore, if she did harm to him,
  That he would strike her dead.

"Oh! quit thy sword, and bend thy bow,
  And give me kisses three;
For though I am a poisonous Worm,
  No hurt I will do to thee.

"Oh! quit thy sword, and bend thy bow,
  And give me kisses three;
If I am not won e'er the sun go down,
  Won I shall never be."

He quitted his sword, he bent his bow,
  He gave her kisses three:
She crept into a hole a Worm,
  But stept out a Lady.

No clothing had this Lady fine,
  To keep her from the cold;
He took his mantle from him about,
  And round her did it fold.

He has taken his mantle from him about,
  And it he wrapt her in,
And they are up to Bambrough Castle,
  As fast as they can win.

PART IV

HIS absence and her serpent-shape,
  The King had long deplored;
He now rejoiced to see them both
  Again to him restored.

The Queen they wanted, whom they found
  All pale and sore afraid,
Because she knew her power must yield
  To Childy Wynd's, who said: —

"Woe be to thee, thou wicked Witch,
  An ill death mayest thou dee;
As thou my sister hast likened,
  So likened shalt thou be.

"I will turn you into a Toad,
  That on the ground doth wend;
And won, won, shalt thou never be,
  Till this world hath an end."

  .   .   .   .

Now on the sand near Ida's tower,
  She crawls a loathsome Toad,
And venom spits on every maid
  She meets upon her road.

The virgins all of Bambrough town,
  Will swear that they have seen
This spiteful Toad, of monstrous size,
  Whilst walking they have been.

All folks believe within the shire,
  This story to be true;
And they all run to Spindleston,
  The cave and trough to view.

This fact now Duncan Frasier,
  Of Cheviot, sings in rhyme,
Lest Bambroughshire men should forget
  Some part of it in time.

MERRY GESTES

A TRAGIC STORY

There lived a sage in days of yore,
And he a handsome pigtail wore;
But wondered much, and sorrowed more,
* Because it hung behind him.*

He mused upon this curious case,
And swore he'd change the pigtail's place,
And have it hanging at his face,
* Not dangling there behind him.*

Says he, " The mystery I've found, —
I'll turn me round," — he turned him round;
* But still it hung behind him.*

Then round and round, and out and in,
All day the puzzled sage did spin;
In vain — it mattered not a pin —
* The pigtail hung behind him.*

And right, and left, and round about,
And up, and down, and in, and out
He turned; but still the pigtail stout
* Hung steadily behind him.*

And though his efforts never slack,
And though he twist, and twirl, and tack,
Alas! still faithful to his back,
* The pigtail hangs behind him.*

William Makepeace Thackeray
From Chamisso

LITTLE BILLEE

THERE were three sailors of Bristol city,
Who took a boat and went to sea.
But first with beef and captain's biscuits
And pickled pork they loaded she.

There was gorging Jack and guzzling Jimmy,
And the youngest he was little Billee.
Now when they got as far as the Equator
They'd nothing left but one split pea.

Says gorging Jack to guzzling Jimmy,
"I am extremely hungaree."
To gorging Jack says guzzling Jimmy,
"We've nothing left, us must eat we."

Says gorging Jack to guzzling Jimmy,
"With one another we should n't agree!
There's little Bill, he's young and tender,
We're old and tough, so let's eat he.

"Oh! Billy, we're going to kill and eat you,
So undo the button of your chemie."
When Bill received this information,
He used his pocket handkerchie.

"First let me say my catechism,
Which my poor mammy taught to me."
"Make haste, make haste," says guzzling Jimmy,
While Jack pulled out his snickersnee.

So Billy went up to the main top-gallant mast,
And down he fell on his bended knee.
He scarce had come to the twelfth commandment
When up he jumps. "There's land I see:

"Jerusalem and Madagascar,
And North and South Amerikee:
There's the British flag a-riding at anchor,
With Admiral Napier, K. C. B."

So when they got aboard of the Admiral's,
He hanged fat Jack and flogged Jimmee;
But as for little Bill he made him
The Captain of a Seventy-three.

William Makepeace Thackeray

BRIAN O'LINN

BRIAN O'LINN was a gentleman born,
His hair it was long and his beard unshorn,
His teeth were out and his eyes far in, —
"I'm a wonderful beauty," says Brian O'Linn!

Brian O'Linn was hard up for a coat,
He borrowed the skin of a neighbouring goat,

He buckled the horns right under his chin, —
"They'll answer for pistols," says Brian O'Linn!

Brian O'Linn had no breeches to wear,
He got him a sheepskin to make him a pair,
With the fleshy side out and the woolly side in, —
"They are pleasant and cool," says Brian O'Linn!

Brian O'Linn had no hat to his head,
He stuck on a pot that was under the shed,
He murdered a cod for the sake of his fin, —
"'T will pass for a feather," says Brian O'Linn!

Brian O'Linn had no shirt to his back,
He went to a neighbour and borrowed a sack,
He puckered a meal-bag under his chin, —
"They'll take it for ruffles," says Brian O'Linn!

Brian O'Linn had no shoes at all,
He bought an old pair at a cobbler's stall,
The uppers were broken and the soles were thin,—
"They'll do me for dancing," says Brian O'Linn!

Brian O'Linn had no watch for to wear,
He bought a fine turnip, and scooped it out fair,
He slipped a live cricket right under the skin, —
"They'll think it is ticking," says Brian O'Linn!

Brian O'Linn was in want of a brooch,
He stuck a brass pin in a big coackroach,

The breast of his shirt he fixed it straight in, —
"They'll think it's a diamond," says Brian
    O'Linn!

Brian O'Linn went a-courting one night,
He set both the mother and daughter to fight,—
"Stop! stop!" he exclaimed, "if you have but the
    tin,
I'll marry you both," says Brian O'Linn!

Brian O'Linn went to bring his wife home,
He had but one horse, that was all skin and bone,
"I'll put her behind me, as nate as a pin,
And her mother before me," says Brian O'Linn.

Brian O'Linn and his wife and wife's mother,
They all crossed over the bridge together,
The bridge broke down and they all tumbled in,—
"We'll go home by water," says Brian O'Linn!

DICKY OF BALLYMAN

On New Year's Day, as I heard say,
Dicky he saddled his dapple grey;
He put on his Sunday clothes,
His scarlet vest, and his new made hose.
    Diddle dum di, diddle dum do,
    Diddle dum di, diddle dum do!

He rode till he came to Wilson Hall,
There he rapped, and loud did call;
Mistress Ann came down straightway,
And asked him what he had to say.

"Don't you know me, Mistress Ann?
I am Dicky of Ballyman;
An honest lad, though I am poor, —
I never was in love before.

"I have an uncle, the best of friends,
Sometimes to me a fat rabbit he sends;
And many other dainty fowl,
To please my life, my joy, my soul.

"Sometimes I reap, sometimes I mow,
And to the market I do go,
To sell my father's corn and hay, —
I earn my sixpence every day!"

"Oh, Dicky! you go beneath your mark, —
You only wander in the dark;
Sixpence a day will never do,
I must have silks, and satins, too!

"Besides, Dicky, I must have tea
For my breakfast, every day;
And after dinner a bottle of wine, —
For without it I cannot dine."

"If on fine clothes our money is spent,
Pray how shall my lord be paid his rent?
He 'll expect it when 't is due, —
Believe me, what I say is true.

"As for tea, good stirabout
Will do far better, I make no doubt;
And spring water, when you dine,
Is far wholesomer than wine.

"Potatoes, too, are very nice food, —
I don't know any half so good:
You may have them boiled or roast,
Whichever way you like them most."

This gave the company much delight,
And made them all to laugh outright;
So Dicky had no more to say,
But saddled his dapple and rode away.
        Diddle dum di, diddle dum do,
        Diddle dum di, diddle dum do!

THE BALLAD OF THE OYSTERMAN

It was a tall young Oysterman lived by the river-
        side,
His shop was just upon the bank, his boat was on
        the tide;

The daughter of a Fisherman, that was so straight
    and slim,
Lived over on the other bank, right opposite to
    him.

It was the pensive Oysterman that saw a lovely
    maid,
Upon a moonlight evening, a-sitting in the shade;
He saw her wave her handkerchief, as much as if
    to say,
"I'm wide awake, young Oysterman, and all the
    folks away."

Then up arose the Oysterman, and to himself
    said he,
"I guess I'll leave the skiff at home, for fear that
    folks should see;
I read it in the story-book, that, for to kiss his
    dear,
Leander swam the Hellespont, — and I will swim
    this here."

And he has leaped into the waves, and crossed
    the shining stream,
And he has clambered up the bank, all in the
    moonlight gleam;
Oh! there were kisses sweet as dew, and words as
    soft as rain, —
But they have heard her father's step, and in he
    leaps again!

Out spoke the ancient Fisherman, — "Oh! what
    was that, my daughter?"
"'T was nothing but a pebble, sir, I threw into
    the water."
"And what is that, pray tell me, love, that
    paddles off so fast?"
"It's nothing but a porpoise, sir, that's been a
    swimming past."

Out spoke the ancient Fisherman, — "Now bring
    me my harpoon!
I'll get into my fishing-boat, and fix the fellow
    soon."
Down fell that pretty innocent, as falls a snow-
    white lamb,
Her hair drooped round her pallid cheeks, like
    seaweed on a clam.

Alas, for those two loving ones! she waked not
    from her swound,
And he was taken with the cramp, and in the
    waves was drowned;
But Fate has metamorphosed them, in pity of
    their woe,
And now they keep an oyster-shop for Mermaids
    down below.

Oliver Wendell Holmes

THE CINDER KING

Who is it that sits in the kitchen and weeps,
While tick goes the clock, and the tabby-cat
        sleeps, —
That watches the grate, without ceasing to spy
Whether purses or coffins will out of it fly?

'T is Betty; who saw the false tailor, Bob Scott,
Lead a bride to the altar, which bride she was not.
'T is Betty, determined love from her to fling,
And woo, for his riches, the dark Cinder-King.

Now spent tallow-candle-grease fattened the soil,
And the blue-burning lamp had half wasted its oil,
And the black-beetle boldly came crawling from
        far,
And the red coals were sinking beneath the third
        bar;

When "*one!*" struck the clock — and instead of
        the bird
Who used to sing cuckoo whene'er the clock stirred,
Out burst a grim raven, and uttered "*caw! caw!*"
While Puss, though she woke, durst not put forth
        a claw.

Then the jack fell a-going as if one should sup,
Then the earth rocked as though it would swallow
        one up;

With fuel from Hell, a strange coal-scuttle came,
And a self-handled poker made fearful the flame.

A cinder shot from it, of size to amaze,
With a bounce, such as Betty ne'er heard in her
　　days,
Thrice, serpent-like, hissed as its heat fled away,
And, lo! something dark in a vast coffin lay!

"Come, Betty," quoth croaking that nondescript
　　thing,
"Come, bless the fond arms of your true Cinder-
　　King!
Three more Kings, my brothers, are waiting to
　　greet ye,
Who — don't take it ill — must at four o'clock
　　eat ye.

"My darling! it must be, do make up your mind;
We element brothers, united, and kind,
Have a feast and a wedding, each night of our
　　lives,
So constantly sup on each other's new wives."

In vain squalled the cook-maid, and prayed not to
　　wed;
Cinder crunched in her mouth, cinder rained on
　　her head.
She sank in the coffin with cinders strewn o'er,
And coffin nor Betty saw man any more.

　　　　　　　　　　　　　Modern, anon.

THE FROLICKSOME DUKE; OR,
THE TINKER'S GOOD FORTUNE

Now, as fame does report, a young Duke keeps a
    Court,
One that pleases his fancy with frolicksome sport:
But amongst all the rest, here is one, I protest,
Which will make you to smile when you hear the
    true jest:
A poor Tinker he found, lying drunk on the
    ground,
As secure in a sleep as if laid in a swound.

The Duke said to his men, "William, Richard,
    and Ben,
Take him home to my palace; we'll sport with him
    then."
O'er a horse he was laid, and with care soon con-
    veyed
To the palace, altho' he was poorly arrai'd:
Then they stript off his cloaths, both his shirt,
    shoes, and hose,
And they put him to bed for to take his repose.

Having pulled off his shirt, which was all over
    durt,
They did give him clean holland, this was no great
    hurt:

On a bed of soft down, like a lord of renown,
They did lay him to sleep the drink out of his
    crown.
In the morning, when day, then admiring he lay,
For to see the rich chamber, both gaudy and gay.

Now he lay something late, in his rich bed of state,
Till at last Knights and Squires they on him did
    wait;
And the chamberling bare, then did likewise de-
    clare,
He desired to know what apparel he'd ware:
The poor Tinker amazed, on the gentleman gazed,
And admired how he to this honour was raised.

Tho' he seemed something mute, yet he chose a
    rich suit,
Which he straitways put on without longer dis-
    pute;
With a star on his side, which the Tinker off 't
    eyed,
And it seemed for to swell him no little with pride;
For he said to himself, "Where is Joan my sweet
    wife?
Sure she never did see me so fine in her life."

From a convenient place, the right Duke, his good
    grace,
Did observe his behaviour in every case.

To a garden of state, on the Tinker they wait,
Trumpets sounding before him: thought he,
     " This is great!"
Where an hour or two, pleasant walks he did view,
With Commanders and Squires in scarlet and
     blew.

A fine dinner was drest, both for him and his guests,
He was placed at the table above all the rest,
In a rich chair or bed lined with fine crimson red,
With a rich golden canopy over his head:
As he sat at his meat, the musick played sweet,
With the choicest of singing his joys to compleat.

While the Tinker did dine, he had plenty of wine,
Rich canary, with sherry and tent superfine.
Like a right honest soul, faith, he took off his bowl.
Till at last he began for to tumble and roul
From his chair to the floor, where he sleeping did
     snore,
Being seven times drunker than ever before.

Then the Duke did ordain, they should strip him
     amain,
And restore him his old leather garments again:
'T was a point next the worst, yet perform it they
     must,
And they carryed him strait where they found him
     at first:

Then he slept all the night, as indeed well he
     might;
But when he did waken, his joys took their flight.

For his glory to him so pleasant did seem,
That he thought it to be but a meer golden dream;
Till at length he was brought to the Duke, where
     he sought
For a pardon, as fearing he had set him at nought:
But his Highness he said, "Thou'rt a jolly bold
     blade:
Such a frolick before, I think, never was plaid."

Then his Highness bespoke him a new suit and
     cloak,
Which he gave for the sake of this frolicksome
     joak:
Nay, and five-hundred pound, with ten acres of
     ground:
"Thou shalt never," said he, "range the counteries
     round,
Crying 'old brass to mend,' for I'll be thy good
     friend,
Nay, and Joan thy sweet wife shall my Duchess
     attend."

Then the Tinker replyed; "What! must Joan my
     sweet bride
Be a Lady in chariots of pleasure to ride?

Must we have gold and land ev'ry day at com-
    mand?
Then I shall be a Squire, I well understand:
Well I thank your good grace, and your love I
    embrace;
I was never before in so happy a case!"

KING JAMES THE FIRST AND THE TINKLER

AND now, to be brief, let's pass over the rest,
Who seldom or never were given to jest,
And come to King Jamie, the first of our throne,
A pleasanter Monarch sure never was known.

As he was a-hunting the swift fallow-deer,
He dropped all his nobles; and when he got clear,
In hope of some pastime away he did ride,
Till he came to an alehouse, hard by a wood-side.

And there with a Tinkler he happened to meet,
And him in kind sort he so freely did greet:
"Pray thee, good fellow, what hast in thy jug,
Which under thy arm thou dost lovingly hug?"

"By the mass!" quoth the Tinkler, "it's nappy
    brown ale,
And for to drink to thee, friend, I will not fail;
For although thy jacket looks gallant and fine,
I think that my twopence as good is as thine."

"By my soul! honest fellow, the truth thou hast
        spoke,"
And straight he sat down with the Tinkler to
        joke;
They drank to the King, and they pledged to each
        other;
Who'd seen 'em had thought they were brother
        and brother.

As they were a-drinking the King pleased to say,
"What news, honest fellow? come tell me, I
        pray?"
"There's nothing of news, beyond that I hear
The King's on the border a-chasing the deer.

"And truly I wish I so happy may be
Whilst he is a-hunting the King I might see;
For although I've travelled the land many ways
I never have yet seen a King in my days."

The King, with a hearty brisk laughter, replied,
"I tell thee, good fellow, if thou canst but ride,
Thou shalt get up behind me, and I will thee bring
To the presence of Jamie, thy sovereign King."

"But he'll be surrounded with nobles so gay,
And how shall we tell him from them, sir, I pray?"
"Thou 'lt easily ken him when once thou art there;
The King will be covered, his nobles all bare."

He got up behind him and likewise his sack,
His budget of leather, and tools at his back;
They rode till they came to the merry Greenwood,
His nobles came round him, bareheaded they
    stood.

The Tinkler then seeing so many appear,
He slily did whisper the King in his ear;
Saying, "They're all clothed so gloriously gay,
But which amongst them is the King, sir, I pray?"

The King did with hearty good laughter, reply,
"By my soul! my good fellow, it's thou or it's I!
The rest are bareheaded, uncovered all round" —
With his bag and his budget he fell to the
    ground,

Like one that was frightened quite out of his wits,
Then on his knees he instartly gets,
Beseeching for mercy; the King to him said,
"Thou art a good fellow, so be not afraid.

"Come, tell thy name." "I am John of the Dale,
A mender of kettles, a lover of ale."
"Rise up, Sir John, I will honour thee here, —
I make thee a Knight of three thousand a year!"

This was a good thing for the Tinkler indeed;
Then unto the Court he was sent for with speed,

Where great store of pleasure and pastime **was**
    seen,
In the royal presence of King and of Queen.

Sir John of the Dale he has land, he has fee,
At the Court of the King who so happy as he?
Yet still in his hall hangs the Tinkler's old **sack**,
And the budget of tools which he bore at his
    back.

KING ALFRED AND THE SHEPHERD

PART I — WHEREIN KING ALFRED FIGHTS FOR HIS DINNER

In elder time there was of yore,
    When gibes of churlish glee
Were used among our country carles,
    Tho' no such thing now be:

The which King Alfred liking well,
    Forsook his stately Court,
And in disguise unknown went forth
    To see that jovial sport;

How Dick and Tom in clouted shoon,
    And coats of russet grey,
Esteemed themselves more brave than them
    That went in golden ray.

In garments fit for such a life
   The good King Alfred went,
Ragged and torn as from his back
   The beggar his clothes had rent.

A sword and buckler good and strong,
   To give Jack Sauce a rap;
And on his head, instead of a crown,
He wore a Monmouth cap.

Thus coasting thorough Somersetshire:
   Near Newton-Court he met
A shepherd swain of lusty limb,
   That up and down did jet:

He wore a bonnet of good grey,
   Close-buttoned to his chin;
And at his back a leather scrip,
   With much good meat therein.

"God speed, good Shepherd," quoth the King
   "I come to be thy guest,
To taste of thy good victuals here,
   And drink that's of the best.

"Thy scrip, I know hath cheer good store":
   "What then?" the Shepherd said,
"Thou seem'st to be some sturdy thief,
   And mak'st me sore afraid.

"Yet if thou wilt thy dinner win,
　　Thy sword and buckler take:
And, if thou canst, into my scrip
　　Therewith an entrance make.

"I tell thee, roister, it hath store
　　Of beef and bacon fat,
With sheaves of barley-bread to make
　　Thy chaps to water at!

"Here stands my bottle, here my bag,
　　If thou canst win them, roister;
Against thy sword and buckler here,
　　My sheep-hook is my master."

"*Benedicite!*" quoth our good King
　　"It never shall be said,
That Alfred, of the Shepherd's hook,
　　Will stand a whit afraid."

So foundly thus they both fell to 't,
　　And giving bang for bang;
At ev'ry blow the Shepherd gave
　　King Alfred's sword cried *twang!*

His buckler proved his chiefest fence;
　　For still the Shepherd's hook
Was that the which King Alfred could
　　In no good manner brook.

At last, when they had fought four hours,
  And it grew just midday,
And wearied both, with right good will,
  Desired each other's stay:

"A truce, I crave," quoth Alfred then
  "Good Shepherd, hold thy hand,
A sturdier fellow than thyself
  Lives not within the land!"

"Nor a lustier roister than thou art,"
  The churlish Shepherd said;
"To tell thee plain, thy thievish look
  Now makes my heart afraid.

"Else sure thou art some prodigal,
  Which hast consumed thy store,
And now com'st wand'ring in this place
  To rob and steal for more."

"Deem not of me, then," quoth our King,
  "Good Shepherd, in this sort.
A gentleman well known I am
  In good King Alfred's Court."

PART II — WHEREIN KING ALFRED BECOMES
A SHEPHERD

"THE DEVIL thou art!" the Shepherd said,
  "Thou go'st in rags all torn;
Thou rather seem'st, I think, to be
  Some beggar basely born.

"But if thou wilt mend thy estate,
 And here a shepherd be;
At night, to Gillian, my sweet wife,
 Thou shalt go home with me:

"For she's as good a toothless dame
 As mumbleth on brown bread;
Where thou shalt lie in hurden sheets,
 Upon a fresh straw bed.

"Of whig and whey we have good store,
 And keep good pease-straw fire;
And now and then good barley cakes,
 As better days require.

"But for my master, which is Chief
 And Lord of Newton-Court,
He keeps, I say, his shepherd swains
 In far more braver sort;

"We there have curds and clouted cream
 Of red cow's morning milk;
And now and then fine buttered cakes
 As soft as any silk.

"Of beef and reifed bacon store,
 That is most fat and greasy,
We have likewise, to feed our chaps
 And make them glib and easy.

"Thus if thou wilt my man become,
   This usage thou shalt have;
If not, adieu; go hang thyself;
   And so farewell, Sir Knave."

King Alfred hearing of this glee
   The churlish Shepherd said,
Was well content to be his man;
   So they a bargain made;

A penny round the Shepherd gave
   In earnest of this match,
To keep his sheep in field and fold,
   As shepherds use to watch.

His wages shall be full ten groats,
   For service of a year,
Yet was it not his use, old lad,
   To hire a man so dear:

"For, did the King himself," quoth he,
   "Unto my cottage come,
He should not, for a twelve-month's pay,
   Receive a greater sum."

PART III — WHEREIN KING ALFRED BURNS THE CAKES

HEREAT the bonny King grew blithe,
   To hear the clownish jest;
How silly sots, as custom is,
   Do descant at the best.

But not to spoil the foolish sport,
 He was content, good King,
To fit the Shepherd's humour right
 In ev'ry kind of thing.

A sheep-hook then, with Patch his dog,
 And tar-box by his side;
He, with his master, cheek by jowl,
 Unto old Gillian hied,

Into whose sight no sooner come,
 "Whom have you here?" quoth she,
"A fellow, I doubt, will cut our throats,
 So like a knave looks he."

"Not so, old Dame," quoth Alfred straight,
 "Of me you need not fear;
My master hired me for ten groats,
 To serve you one whole year:

"So, good Dame Gillian, grant me leave
 Within your house to stay;
For, by St. Anne, do what you can,
 I will not yet away."

Her churlish usage pleased him still,
 And put him to such proof,
That he at night was almost choked
 Within that smoky roof.

But as he sat with smiling cheer
  The event of all to see,
His dame brought forth a piece of dough
  Which in the fire throws she.

Where lying on the hearth to bake,
  By chance, the cake did burn:
"What! canst thou not, thou lout," quoth she,
  "Take pains the same to turn?

"Thou art more quick to take it out,
  And eat it up half dough,
Than thus to stay till't be enough,
  And so thy manners show!

"But serve me such another trick,
  I'll thwack thee on the snout:"
Which made the patient King, poor man,
  Of her to stand in doubt.

PART IV — WHEREIN KING ALFRED BLOWS HIS
BUGLE-HORN

BUT, to be brief, to bed they went
  The old man and his wife;
But never such a lodging had
  King Alfred in his life!

For he was laid in white sheep's wool,
  New-pulled from tanned fells;
And o'er his head hanged spiders' webs
  As if they had been bells.

"Is this the country guise?" thought he,
  "Then here I will not stay,
But hence be gone, as soon as breaks
  The peeping of next day!"

The cackling hens and geese kept roost,
  And perched at his side;
Where, at the last, the watchful cock
  Made known the morning tide.

Then up got Alfred, with his horn,
  And blew so long a blast,
That it made Gillian and her groom,
  In bed, full sore aghast.

"Arise," quoth she, "We are undone!
  This night we lodged have,
At unawares, within our house,
  A false dissembling knave.

"Rise! husband, rise! he'll cut our throats!
  He calleth for his mates.
I'd give, old Will, our good cade lamb,
  He would depart our gates!"

But still King Alfred blew his horn,
  Before them, more and more,
Till that an hundred Lords and Knights
  All lighted at the door.

Who cried, "All hail! all hail, good King!
  Long have we sought your Grace!"
"And here you find, my merry men all,
  Your Sov'reign in this place."

"We surely must be hanged up both,
  Old Gillian, I much fear,"
The Shepherd said, "for using thus,
  Our good King Alfred here."

"Oh, pardon, my Liege!" quoth Gillian then,
  "For my husband, and for me.
By these ten bones, I never thought
  The same that now I see!"

"And by my hook," the Shepherd said,
  "An oath both good and true!
Before this time, O noble King,
  I ne'er your Highness knew!

"Then pardon me and my old wife,
  That we may after say,
When first you came into our house,
  It was a happy day."

"It shall be done," said Alfred straight,
  "And Gillian, thy old dame,
For this her churlish using me,
  Deserveth not much blame;

"For 'tis thy country guise, I see,
  To be thus bluntish still,
And where the plainest meaning is,
  Remains the smallest ill.

"And, Master, lo! I tell thee now;
  For thy late manhood shown,
A thousand wethers I'll bestow
  Upon thee, for thy own;

"And pasture-ground, as much as will
  Suffice to feed them all:
And this thy cottage, I will change
  Into a stately hall."

"And for the same, as duty binds,"
  The Shepherd said, "good King,
A milk-white lamb, once ev'ry year,
  I'll to your Highness bring:

"And Gillian, my wife, likewise,
  Of wool to make you coats,
Will give you as much at New Year's tide,
  As shall be worth ten groats.

"And in your praise my bag-pipes shall
  Sound sweetly once a year,
How Alfred, our renowned King,
  Most kindly hath been here."

"Thanks, Shepherd, thanks," quoth he again:
  "The next time I come hither,
My Lords with me, here in this house,
  Will all be merry together."

SAD GESTES

THE SANDS OF DEE

"*O Mary, go and call the cattle home,*
And call the cattle home,
And call the cattle home
Across the sands of Dee;"
The western wind was wild and dank wi' foam,
And all alone went she.

The western tide crept up along the sand,
And o'er and o'er the sand,
And round and round the sand,
As far as eye could see.
The rolling mist came down and hid the land —
And never home came she.

"*Oh! is it weed, or fish, or floating hair —*
A tress o' golden hair,
A drowned maiden's hair
Above the nets at sea?
Was never salmon yet that shone so fair
Among the stakes on Dee."

They rowed her in across the rolling foam,
The cruel crawling foam,
The cruel hungry foam
To her grave beside the sea:
But still the boatmen hear her call the cattle home
Across the sands of Dee!

Charles Kingsley

FAIR ANNY OF ROCH-ROYAL

PART I

"O WHA will shoe my fu fair foot?
    An wha will glove my han?
An wha will lace my middle gimp
    Wi the new made London ban?

"Or wha will kemb my yallow hair,
    Wi the new made silver kemb?
Or wha'll be father to my young bairn,
    Till Love Gregor come hame?"

Her father shoed her fu fair foot,
    Her mother glovd her han;
Her sister lac'd her middle gimp
    Wi the new made London ban.

Her brother kembd her yallow hair,
    Wi the new made silver kemb,
But the king o heaven maun father her bairn,
    Till Love Gregor come hame.

"O gin I had a bony ship,
    An men to sail wi me,
It's I would gang to my true-love,
    Since he winna come to me."

Her father's gien her a bonny ship,
　An sent her to the stran;
She's tane her young son in her arms,
　An turnd her back to the lan.

She had na been o the sea saillin
　About a month or more,
Till landed has she her bonny ship
　Near her true-love's door.

The night was dark, an the win blew caul,
　An her love was fast asleep,
An the bairn that was in her twa arms
　Fu sair began to weep.

Long stood she at her true-love's door,
　An lang tirld at the pin;
At length up gat his fa'se mither,
　Says, "Wha's that woud be in?"

"O it is Anny of Roch-royal,
　Your love, come oer the sea,
But an your young son in her arms;
　So open the door to me."

"Awa, awa, you ill woman,
　You've na come here for gude;
You're but a witch, or wile warlock,
　Or mermaid o the flude."

"I'm na a witch, or wile warlock,
    Nor mermaiden," said she;
"I'm but Fair Anny o Roch-royal;
    O open the door to me."

"O gin ye be Anny o Roch-royal,
    As I trust not ye be,
What taiken can ye gie that ever
    I kept your company?"

"O dinna ye mind, Love Gregor," she says,
    "Whan we sat at the wine,
How we changed the napkins frae our necks,
    It's na sae lang sin syne?

"An yours was good, an good enough,
    But nae sae good as mine;
For yours was o the cumbruk clear,
    But mine was silk sae fine.

"An dinna ye mind, Love Gregor," she says,
    "As we twa sat at dine,
How we changed the rings frae our fingers,
    But ay the best was mine?

"For yours was good, an good enough,
    Yet nae sae good as mine;
For yours was of the good red gold,
    But mine o the diamonds fine.

"Sae open the door now, Love Gregor,
  An open it wi speed,
Or your young son that is in my arms
  For cauld will soon be dead."

"Awa, awa, you ill woman,
  Gae frae my door for shame;
For I hae gotten another fair love,
  Sae ye may hye you hame."

"O hae you gotten another fair love,
  For a' the oaths you sware?
Then fair you well now, fa'se Gregor,
  For me you's never see mair."

O heely, heely gi'd she back,
  As the day began to peep;
She set her foot on good ship-board,
  An sair, sair did she weep.

PART II

LOVE GREGOR started frae his sleep,
  An to his mither did say,
"I dreamd a dream this night, mither,
  That maks my heart right wae.

"I dreamd that Anny of Roch-royal,
  The flowr o a' her kin,
Was standin mournin at my door,
  But nane would lat her in."

"O there was a woman stood at the door,
  Wi a bairn intill her arms,
But I woud na lat her within the bowr,
  For fear she had done you harm."

O quickly, quickly raise he up,
  An fast ran to the stran,
An there he saw her Fair Anny,
  Was sailin frae the lan.

An "Heigh, Anny!" an "Hou, Anny!
  O Anny, speak to me!"
But ay the louder that he cried "Anny,"
  The louder roard the sea.

An "Heigh, Anny!" an "Hou, Anny!
  O Anny, winna you bide?"
But ay the langer that he cried "Anny,"
  The higher roard the tide.

The win grew loud, an the sea grew rough,
  An the ship was rent in twain,
An soon he saw her Fair Anny
  Come floating oer the main.

He saw his young son in her arms,
  Baith tossd aboon the tide;
He wrang his hands, than fast he ran,
  An plung'd i the sea sae wide.

He catchd her by the yellow hair,
  An drew her to the strand,
But cauld an stiff was every limb
  Before he reachd the land.

O first he kissd her cherry cheek,
  An then he kissd her chin;
An sair he kissd her ruby lips,
  But there was nae breath within.

O he has mournd oer Fair Anny
  Till the sun was gaing down,
Then wi a sigh his heart it brast,
  An his soul to heaven has flown.

THE CRUEL SISTER

THERE were two sisters sat in a bour,
        Binnorie, O Binnorie;
There came a knight to be their wooer;
        By the bonny milldams of Binnorie.

He courted the eldest with glove and ring,
        Binnorie, O Binnorie;
But he lo'ed the youngest abune a' thing;
        By the bonny milldams of Binnorie.

He courted the eldest with broach and knife,
        Binnorie, O Binnorie;
But he lo'ed the youngest abune his life;
        By the bonny milldams of Binnorie.

The eldest she was vexed sair,
             Binnorie, O Binnorie;
And sore envied her sister fair;
             By the bonny milldams of Binnorie.

The eldest said to the youngest ane,
             Binnorie, O Binnorie;
"Will ye go and see your father's ships come in?"—
             By the bonny milldams of Binnorie.

She's ta'en her by the lily hand,
             Binnorie, O Binnorie;
And led her down to the river strand;
             By the bonny milldams of Binnorie.

The youngest stude upon a stane,
             Binnorie, O Binnorie;
The eldest came and pushed her in;
             By the bonny milldams of Binnorie.

She took her by the middle sma',
             Binnorie, O Binnorie;
And dash'd her bonny back to the jaw;
             By the bonny milldams of Binnorie.

"O sister, sister, reach your hand,
             Binnorie, O Binnorie;
Ard ye shall be heir of half my land." —
             By the bonny milldams of Binnorie.

"O sister, I'll not reach my hand,
            Binnorie, O Binnorie;
And I'll be heir of all your land;
            By the bonny milldams of **Binnorie.**

"Shame fa' the hand that I should take,
            Binnorie, O Binnorie;
It's twin'd me, and my world's make." —
            By the bonny milldams of Binnorie.

"O sister, reach me but your glove,
            Binnorie, O Binnorie;
And sweet William shall be your love." —
            By the bonny milldams of Binnorie.

"Sink on, nor hope for hand or glove!
            Binnorie, O Binnorie:
And sweet William shall better be my love,
            By the bonny milldams of Binnorie.

"Your cherry cheeks and your yellow hair,
            Binnorie, O Binnorie;
Garr'd me gang maiden evermair." —
            By the bonny milldams of **Binnorie.**

Sometimes she sunk, and sometimes she swam,
            Binnorie, O Binnorie;
Until she cam to the miller's dam;
            By the bonny milldams of **Binnorie.**

"O father, father, draw your dam!
          Binnorie, O Binnorie;
There's either a mermaid, or a milk-white
     swan." —
          By the bonny milldams of Binnorie.

The miller hasted and drew his dam,
          Binnorie, O Binnorie;
And there he found a drown'd woman;
          By the bonny milldams of Binnorie.

You could not see her yellow hair,
          Binnorie, O Binnorie;
For gowd and pearls that were sae rare;
          By the bonny milldams of Binnorie.

You could na see her middle sma'.
          Binnorie, O Binnorie;
Her gowden girdle was sae bra';
          By the bonny milldams of Binnorie.

A famous harper passing by,
          Binnorie, O Binnorie;
The sweet pale face he chanced to spy;
          By the bonny milldams of Binnorie.

And when he looked that lady on,
          Binnorie, O Binnorie;
He sigh'd and made a heavy moan;
          By the bonny milldams of Binnorie.

He made a harp of her breast-bone,
              Binnorie, O Binnorie;
Whose sounds would melt a heart of stone;
              By the bonny milldams of Binnorie.

The strings he framed of her yellow hair,
              Binnorie, O Binnorie;
Whose notes made sad the listening ear;
              By the bonny milldams of Binnorie.

He brought it to her father's hall,
              Binnorie, O Binnorie;
And there was the court assembled all;
              By the bonny milldams of Binnorie.

He laid this harp upon a stone,
              Binnorie, O Binnorie;
And straight it began to play alone!
              By the bonny milldams of Binnorie.

"O yonder sits my father, the king,
              Binnorie, O Binnorie;
And yonder sits my mother, the queen;
              By the bonny milldams of Binnorie.

"And yonder stands my brother Hugh,
              Binnorie, O Binnorie;
And by him my William, sweet and true." —
              By the bonny milldams of Binnorie.

But the last tune that the harp play'd then,
  Binnorie, O Binnorie;
Was — "Woe to my sister, false Helen!" —
  By the bonny milldams of Binnorie.

BARBARA ALLEN'S CRUELTY

In Scarlet Town, where I was bound,
  There was a fair maid dwelling,
Whom I had chosen to be my own,
  And her name it was Barbara Allen.

All in the merry month of May,
  When green leaves they was springing,
This young man on his death-bed lay,
  For the love of Barbara Allen.

He sent his man unto her then,
  To the town where she was dwelling:
"You must come to my master dear,
  If your name be Barbara Allen.

"For death is printed in his face,
  And sorrow's in him dwelling,
And you must come to my master dear,
  If your name be Barbara Allen."

"If death be printed in his face,
  And sorrow's in him dwelling,
Then little better shall he be
  For bonny Barbara Allen."

So slowly, slowly she got up,
　And so slowly she came to him,
And all she said when she came there,
　"Young man, I think you are a dying."

He turnd his face unto her then:
　"If you be Barbara Allen,
My dear," said he, "come pitty me,
　As on my death-bed I am lying."

"If on your death-bed you be lying,
　What is that to Barbara Allen?
I cannot keep you from your death;
　So farewell," said Barbara Allen.

He turnd his face unto the wall,
　And death came creeping to him:
"Then adieu, adieu, and adieu to all,
　And adieu to Barbara Allen!"

And as she was walking on a day,
　She heard the bell a ringing,
And it did seem to ring to her
　"Unworthy Barbara Allen."

She turnd herself round about,
　And she spy'd the corps a coming:
"Lay down, lay down the corps of clay,
　That I may look upon him."

And all the while she looked on,
  So loudly she lay laughing,
While all her friends cry'd out amain,
  "Unworthy Barbara Allen!"

When he was dead, and laid in grave,
  Then death came creeping to she:
"O mother, mother, make my bed,
  For his death hath quite undone me.

"A hard-hearted creature that I was,
  To slight one that lovd me so dearly;
I wish I had been more kinder to him,
  The time of his life when he was near me."

So this maid she then did dye,
  And desired to be buried by him,
And repented her self before she dy'd,
  That ever she did deny him.

SONG: EARL MARCH LOOKED ON
HIS DYING CHILD

EARL MARCH looked on his dying child,
  And, smit with grief to view her,
"The youth," he cried, "whom I exiled
  Shall be restored to woo her."

She's at the window many an hour
  His coming to discover:
And her Love looked up to Ellen's bower,
  And she looked on her Lover. —

But ah! so pale, he knew her not,
   Though her smile on him was dwelling.
"And am I then forgot — forgot?"
   It broke the heart of Ellen.

In vain he weeps, in vain he sighs;
   Her cheek is cold as ashes;
Nor Love's own kiss shall wake those eyes
   To lift their silken lashes.

                Thomas Campbell

LORD LOVEL

LORD LOVEL he stood at his castle gate,
   Combing his milk-white steed;
When up came Lady Nancy Belle,
   To wish her lover good speed, speed,
   To wish her lover good speed.

"Where are you going, Lord Lovel?" she said,
   "Oh! where are you going?" said she;
"I'm going, my Lady Nancy Belle,
   Strange countries for to see, to see,
   Strange countries for to see."

"When will you be back, Lord Lovel?" she said;
   "Oh! when will you come back?" said she;
"In a year or two — or three, at the most,
   I'll return to my fair Nancy-cy,
   I'll return to my fair Nancy."

But he had not been gone a year and a day,
    Strange countries for to see,
When languishing thoughts came into his head,
    Lady Nancy Belle he would go see, see,
    Lady Nancy Belle he would go see.

So he rode, and he rode on his milk-white steed,
    Till he came to London-town;
And there he heard St. Pancras' bells,
    And the people all mourning round, round,
    And the people all mourning round.

"Oh! what is the matter?" Lord Lovel he said,
    "Oh! what is the matter?" said he;
"A Lord's Lady is dead," a woman replied,
    "And some call her Lady Nancy-cy,
    And some call her Lady Nancy."

So he ordered the grave to be opened wide,
    And the shroud he turned down,
And there he kissed her clay-cold lips,
    Till the tears came trickling down, down,
    Till the tears came trickling down.

Lady Nancy she died as it might be to-day,
    Lord Lovel he died as to-morrow;
Lady Nancy she died out of pure, pure grief,
    Lord Lovel he died out of sorrow, sorrow,
    Lord Lovel he died out of sorrow.

Lady Nancy was laid in St. Pancras' church,
    Lord Lovel was laid in the choir;
And out of her bosom there grew a red rose,
    And out of her lover's a brier, brier,
    And out of her lover's a brier.

They grew, and they grew, to the church steeple,
        too,
    And then they could grow no higher;
So there they entwined in a true lover's knot,
    For all lovers true to admire-mire,
    For all lovers true to admire.

PRETTY MAYS AND KNIGHTS SO BOLD

THE NOBLE RIDDLE

*"If thou canst answer me questions **three**,*
This very day will I marry thee."

"Kind sir, in love, O then," quoth she,
"Tell me what your three questions be."

"O what is longer than the way,
Or what is deeper than the sea?

"Or what is louder than the horn,
Or what is sharper than a thorn?

"Or what is greener than the grass,
Or what is worse than a woman was?"

"O love is longer than the way,
And hell is deeper than the sea.

"And thunder is louder than the horn,
And hunger is sharper than a thorn.

"And poyson is greener than the grass,
And the Devil is worse than woman was."

When she these questions answered had,
The knight became exceeding glad.

And having truly try'd her wit,
He much commended her for it.

And after, as it is verifi'd,
He made of her his lovely bride.

So now, fair maidens all, adieu,
This song I dedicate to you.

I wish that you may constant prove
Vnto the man that you do love.

BLANCHEFLOUR AND JELLY-FLORICE

PART I

THERE was a maid, richly arrayd,
  In robes were rare to see,
For seven years and something mair
  She servd a gay ladie.

But being fond o a higher place,
  In service she thought lang;
She took her mantle her about,
  Her coffer by the band.

And as she walkd by the shore-side,
  As blythe's a bird on tree,
Yet still she gaz'd her round about,
  To see what she could see.

At last she spied a little castle,
  That stood near by the sea;
She spied it far and drew it near,
  To that castle went she.

And when she came to that castle
  She tirled at the pin,
And ready stood a little wee boy
  To lat this fair maid in.

"O who's the owner of this place,
  O porter-boy, tell me;"
"This place belongs unto a queen
  O birth and high degree."

She put her hand in her pocket,
  And gae him shillings three:
"O porter, bear my message well
  Unto the queen frae me."

The porter's gane before the queen,
  Fell low down on his knee:
"Win up, win up, my porter-boy,
  What makes this courtesie?"

"I hae been porter at your yetts,
  My dame, these years full three,
But see a ladie at your yetts
  The fairest my eyes did see."

"Cast up my yetts baith wide and braid,
  Lat her come in to me,
And I'll know by her courtesie
  Lord's daughter if she be."

When she came in before the queen,
  Fell low down on her knee:
"Service frae you, my dame the queen,
  I pray you grant it me."

"If that service ye now do want,
    What station will ye be?
Can ye card wool, or spin, fair maid,
    Or milk the cows to me?"

"No, I can neither card nor spin,
    Nor cows I canno milk,
But sit into a lady's bower
    And sew the seams o silk."

"What is your name, ye comely dame?
    Pray tell this unto me:"
"O Blancheflour, that is my name,
    Born in a strange countrie."

"O keep ye well frae Jellyflorice —
    My ain dear son is he —
When other ladies get a gift,
    O that ye shall get three."

PART II

It wasna tald into the bower
    Till it went thro the ha,
That Jellyflorice and Blancheflour
    Were grown ower great witha.

When the queen's maids their visits paid,
    Upo the gude Yule-day,
When other ladies got horse to ride,
    She boud take foot and gae.

The queen she calld her stable-groom,
    To come to her right seen;
Says, "Ye'll take out yon wild waith steed
    And bring him to the green.

"Ye'll take the bridle frae his head,
    The lighters frae his een;
Ere she ride three times roun the cross,
    Her weel-days will be dune."

Jellyflorice his true-love spy'd
    As she rade roun the cross,
And thrice he kissd her lovely lips,
    And took her frae her horse.

" Gang to your bower, my lily-flower,
    For a' my mother's spite;
There's nae other amang her maids,
    In whom I take delight.

"Ye are my jewel, and only ane,
    Nane's do you injury;
For ere this-day-month come and gang
    My wedded wife ye'se be."

GLENARA

Oh! heard ye yon pibroch sound sad in the gale,
Where a band cometh slowly with weeping and
        wail?

'T is the Chief of Glenara laments for his dear,
And her sire and the people are called to her bier.

Glenara came first, with the mourners and shroud;
Her kinsmen they followed, but mourned not
    aloud.
Their plaids all their bosoms were folded around;
They marched all in silence, — they looked on
    the ground.

In silence they reached, over mountain and moor,
To a heath, where the oak-tree grew lonely and
    hoar;
"Now here let us place the grey stone of her
    cairn;
Why speak ye no word?" — said Glenara the
    stern.

"And tell me, I charge you! ye clan of my spouse,
Why fold ye your mantles, why cloud ye your
    brows?"
So spake the rude chieftain: — no answer is made,
But each mantle unfolding a dagger displayed.

"I dreamt of my lady, I dreamt of her shroud,"
Cried a voice from the kinsmen all, wrathful and
    loud:
"And empty that shroud and that coffin did seem;
Glenara! Glenara! now read me my dream!"

Oh! pale grew the cheek of that chieftain, I ween,
When the shroud was unclosed and no lady was
      seen;
When a voice from the kinsmen spoke louder in
      scorn, —
'T was the youth who had loved the fair Ellen of
      Lorn, —

"I dreamt of my lady, I dreamt of her grief;
I dreamt that her lord was a barbarous Chief;
On a rock of the ocean fair Ellen did seem;
Glenara! Glenara! now read me my dream!"

In dust low the traitor has knelt to the ground;
And the desert revealed where his lady was found;
From a rock of the ocean that beauty is borne, —
Now joy to the house of fair Ellen of Lorn!
               Thomas Campbell

THE BEGGAR-MAID

Her arms across her breast she laid;
  She was more fair than words can say;
Barefooted came the Beggar-maid
  Before the King Cophetua.

In robe and crown the King stept down,
  To meet and greet her on her way;
"It is no wonder," said the Lords,
  "She is more beautiful than day."

As shines the moon in clouded skies,
  She in her poor attire was seen;
One praised her ankles, one her eyes,
  One her dark hair and lovesome mien.

So sweet a face, such angel grace,
  In all that land had never been.
Cophetua sware a royal oath:
  "This Beggar-maid shall be my Queen!"
                    Alfred, Lord Tennyson

LOCHINVAR

Oh! young Lochinvar is come out of the West;
Through all the wide border his steed was the
      best;
And save his good broadsword he weapons had
      none,
He rode all unarmed, and he rode all alone.
So faithful in love, and so dauntless in war,
There never was Knight like the young Lochinvar.

He staid not for brake, and he stopped not for
      stone,
He swam the Eske river where ford there was
      none;
But ere he alighted at Netherby gate,
The bride had consented, the gallant came late;
For a laggard in love, and a dastard in war,
Was to wed the fair Ellen of brave Lochinvar.

So boldly he entered the Netherby Hall,
Among bridesmen, and kinsmen, and brothers
        and all,
Then spoke the bride's father, his hand on his
        sword,
—For the poor craven bridegroom said never a
        word —
"Oh! come ye in peace here, or come ye in war,
Or to dance at our bridal, young Lord Lochin-
        var?"

"I long wooed your daughter, my suit you de-
        nied; —
Love swells like the Solway, but ebbs like its
        tide —
And now am I come with this lost love of mine,
To lead but one measure, drink one cup of wine,
There are maidens in Scotland more lovely by far,
That would gladly be bride to the young Lochin-
        var."

The bride kissed the goblet; the Knight took it up,
He quaffed off the wine, and he threw down the
        cup.
She looked down to blush, and she looked up to
        sigh,
With a smile on her lips, and a tear in her eye.
He took her soft hand, ere her mother could bar,—
"Now tread we a measure," said young Lochinvar.

So stately his form, and so lovely her face,
That never a hall such a galliard did grace;
While her mother did fret, and her father did fume,
And the bridegroom stood dangling his bonnet
    and plume;
And the bride-maidens whispered, " 'T were bet-
    ter by far,
To have matched our fair cousin with young
    Lochinvar."

One touch to her hand, and one word in her ear,
When they reached the hall-door, and the charger
    stood near;
So light to the croupe the fair lady he swung,
So light to the saddle before her he sprung!
"She is won! we are gone, over bank, bush, and
    scaur;
They'll have fleet steeds that follow," quoth
    young Lochinvar.

There was mounting 'mong Græmes of the
    Netherby clan;
Forsters, Fenwicks, and Musgraves, they rode
    and they ran;
There was racing and chasing on Cannobie Lea,
But the lost bride of Netherby ne'er did they see.
So daring in love, and so dauntless in war,
Have ye e'er heard of gallant like young Loch-
    invar?

                        Sir Walter Scott

THE GAY GOSS-HAWK

PART I

"O WALY, waly, my gay goss-hawk,
  Gin your feathering be sheen!" —
"And waly, waly, my master dear,
  Gin ye look pale and lean!

"O have ye tint, at tournament,
  Your sword, or yet your spear;
Or mourn ye for the southern lass,
  Whom ye may not win near?" —

"I have not tint, at tournament,
  My sword, nor yet my spear;
But sair I mourn for my true love,
  Wi' mony a bitter tear.

"But weel's me on ye, my gay goss-hawk,
  Ye can baith speak and flee;
Ye sall carry a letter to my love,
  Bring an answer back to me." —

"But how sall I your true love find,
  Or how suld I her know?
I bear a tongue ne'er wi' her spake,
  An eye that ne'er her saw."

"O weel sall ye my true love ken,
  Sae sune as ye her see;
For, of a' the flowers of fair England,
  The fairest flower is she.

"The red that's on my true love's cheek,
  Is like blood-drops on the snaw;
The white that is on her breast bare,
  Like the down o' the white sea-maw.

"And even at my love's bour-door
  There grows a flowering birk;
And ye maun sit and sing thereon
  As she gangs to the kirk.

"And four-and-twenty fair ladyes
  Will to the mass repair;
But weel may ye my ladye ken,
  The fairest ladye there."

PART II

LORD WILLIAM has written a love-letter,
  Put it under his pinion gray;
And he is awa to Southern land
  As fast as wings can gae.

And even at that ladye's bour
  There grew a flowering birk;
And he sat down and sung thereon
  As she gaed to the kirk.

And weel he kent that ladye fair
  Amang her maidens free;
For the flower, that springs in May morning,
  Was not sae sweet as she.

He lighted at the ladye's yate,
  And sat him on a pin;
And sang fu' sweet the notes o' love,
  Till a' was cosh within.

And first he sang a low low note,
  And syne he sang a clear;
And aye the o'erword o' the sang
  Was — "Your love can no win here."

"Feast on, feast on, my maidens a',
  The wine flows you amang,
While I gang to my shot-window,
  And hear yon bonny bird's sang.

"Sing on, sing on, my bonny bird,
  The sang ye sung yestreen;
For weel I ken, by your sweet singing,
  Ye are frae my true love sen."

O first he sang a merry sang,
  And syne he sang a grave;
And syne he pecked his feathers gray,
  To her the letter gave.

"Have there a letter from lord William;
  He says he's sent ye three;
He canna wait your love langer,
  But for your sake he'll dee." —

"Gae bid him bake his bridal bread,
  And brew his bridal ale;
And I shall meet him at Mary's kirk,
  Lang, lang ere it be stale."

The lady's gane to her chamber,
  And a moanfu' woman was she;
As gin she had ta'en a sudden brash,
  And were about to dee.

"A boon, a boon, my father dear,
  A boon I beg of thee!" —
"Ask not that paughty Scottish lord,
  For him you ne'er shall see.

"But, for your honest asking else,
  Weel granted it shall be." —
"Then, gin I die in Southern land,
  In Scotland gar bury me.

"And the first kirk that ye come to,
  Ye's gar the mass be sung;
And the next kirk that ye come to,
  Ye's gar the bells be rung.

"And when ye come to St. Mary's kirk,
  Ye's tarry there till night."
And so her father pledg'd his word,
  And so his promise plight.

PART III

She has ta'en her to her bigly bour
  As fast as she could fare;
And she has drank a sleepy draught,
  That she had mix'd wi' care.

And pale, pale grew her rosy cheek,
  That was sae bright of blee,
And she seem'd to be as surely dead
  As any one could be.

Then spak her cruel step-minnie,
  "Tak ye the burning lead,
And drap a drap on her bosome,
  To try if she be dead."

They took a drap o' boiling lead,
  They drapp'd it on her breast;
"Alas! alas!" her father cried,
  "She's dead without the priest."

She neither chatter'd with her teeth,
  Nor shiver'd with her chin;
"Alas! alas!" her father cried,
  "There is nae breath within."

Then up arose her seven brethren,
   And hew'd to her a bier;
They hew'd it frae the solid aik,
   Laid it o'er wi' silver clear.

Then up and gat her seven sisters,
   And sewed to her a kell;
And every steek that they put in
   Sewed to a siller bell.

The first Scots kirk that they cam to,
   They garr'd the bells be rung;
The next Scots kirk that they cam to,
   They garr'd the mass be sung.

But when they cam to St. Mary's kirk,
   There stude spearmen all on a raw;
And up and started lord William,
   The chieftane amang them a'.

"Set down, set down the bier," he said,
   "Let me look her upon:"
But as soon as lord William touch'd her hand,
   Her colour began to come.

She brightened like the lily flower,
   Till her pale colour was gone;
With rosy cheik, and ruby lip,
   She smiled her love upon.

"A morsel of your bread, my lord,
   And one glass of your wine;
For I hae fasted these three lang days,
   All for your sake and mine. —

"Gae hame, gae hame, my seven bauld brothers,
   Gae hame and blaw your horn!
I trow ye wad hae gi'en me the skaith,
   But I've gi'en you the scorn.

"Commend me to my gray father,
   That wished my saul gude rest;
But wae be to my cruel step-dame,
   Garr'd burn me on the breast." —

"Ah! woe to you, you light woman!
   An ill death may you dee!
For we left father and sisters at hame
   Breaking their hearts for thee."

BONNY BABY LIVINGSTON

PART I

O BONNY Baby Livingston
   Went forth to view the hay,
And by it came him Glenlion,
   Sta bonny Baby away.

O first he's taen her silken coat,
  And neest her satten gown,
Syne rowd her in a tartan plaid,
  And hapd her round and rown.

He has set her upon his steed
  And roundly rode away,
And neer loot her look back again
  The live-long summer's day.

He's carried her oer hills and muirs
  Till they came to a Highland glen,
And there he's met his brother John,
  With twenty armed men.

O there were cows, and there were ewes,
  And lasses milking there,
But Baby neer anse lookd about,
  Her heart was filld wi care.

Glenlion took her in his arms,
  And kissd her, cheek and chin;
Says, " I 'd gie a' these cows and ewes
  But ae kind look to win."

"O ae kind look ye neer shall get,
  Nor win a smile frae me,
Unless to me you 'll favour shew,
  And take me to Dundee."

"Dundee, Baby? Dundee, Baby?
   Dundee you neer shall see
Till I've carried you to Glenlion
   And have my bride made thee.

"We'll stay a while at Auchingour,
   And get sweet milk and cheese,
And syne we'll gang to Glenlion,
   And there live at our ease."

"I winna stay at Auchingour,
   Nor eat sweet milk and cheese,
Nor go with thee to Glenlion,
   For there I'll neer find ease."

Than out it spake his brother John,
   "O were I in your place,
I'd take that lady hame again,
   For a' her bonny face.

"Commend me to the lass that's kind,
   Tho na so gently born;
And, gin her heart I coudna gain,
   To take her hand I'd scorn."

"O had your tongue now, John," he says,
   "You wis na what you say;
For I've lood that bonny face
   This twelve month and a day.

"And tho I've lood her lang and sair
   A smile I neer coud win;
Yet what I've got anse in my power
   To keep I think nae sin."

PART II

WHEN they came to Glenlion castle,
   They lighted at the yate,
And out it came his sisters three,
   Wha did them kindly greet.

O they've taen Baby by the hands
   And led her oer the green,
And ilka lady spake a word,
   But bonny Baby spake nane.

Then out it spake her bonny Jean,
   The youngest o the three,
"O lady, dinna look sae sad,
   But tell your grief to me."

" O wherefore should I tell my grief,
   Since lax I canna find?
I'm stown frae a' my kin and friends,
   And my love I left behind.

"But had I paper, pen, and ink,
   Before that it were day,
I yet might get a letter sent
   In time to Johny Hay."

O she's got paper, pen, and ink,
    And candle that she might see,
And she has written a broad letter
    To Johny at Dundee.

And she has gotten a bonny boy,
    That was baith swift and strang,
Wi philabeg and bonnet blue,
    Her errand for to gang.

"O boy, gin ye'd my blessing win
    And help me in my need,
Run wi this letter to my love,
    And bid him come wi speed.

"And here's a chain of good red gowd,
    And gowdn guineas three,
And when you've well your errand done,
    You'll get them for your fee."

The boy he ran oer hill and dale,
    Fast as a bird coud flee,
And eer the sun was twa hours height
    The boy was at Dundee.

And when he came to Johny's door
    He knocked loud and sair;
Then Johny to the window came,
    And loudly cry'd, "Wha's there?"

"O here's a letter I have brought,
  Which ye maun quickly read,
And, gin ye woud your lady save,
  Gang back wi me wi speed."

O when he had the letter read,
  An angry man was he;
He says, " Glenlion, thou shalt rue
  · This deed of villany!

" O saddle to me the black, the black,
  O saddle to me the brown,
O saddle to me the swiftest steed
  That eer rade frae the town.

"And arm ye well, my merry men a',
  And follow me to the glen,
For I vow I'll neither eat nor sleep
  Till I get my love again."

He's mounted on a milk-white steed,
  The boy upon a gray,
And they got to Glenlion's castle
  About the close of day.

As Baby at her window stood,
  The west wind saft did bla;
She heard her Johny's well-kent voice
  Beneath the castle wa.

"O Baby, haste, the window jump!
    I'll kep you in my arm;
My merry men a' are at the yate,
    To rescue you frae harm."

She to the window fixt her sheets
    And slipped safely down,
And Johny catchd her in his arms,
    Neer loot her touch the ground.

When mounted on her Johny's horse,
    Fou blithely did she say,
"Glenlion, you hae lost your bride!
    She's aff wi Johny Hay."

PART III

GLENLION and his brother John
    Were birling in the ha,
When they heard Johny's bridle ring,
    As first he rade awa.

"Rise, Jock, gang out and meet the priest,
    I hear his bridle ring;
My Baby now shall be my wife
    Before the laverocks sing."

"O brother, this is not the priest;
    I fear he'll come oer late;
For armed men with shining brands
    Stand at the castle-yate."

"Haste Donald, Duncan, Dugald, Hugh!
　Haste, take your sword and spier!
We'll gar these traytors rue the hour
　That eer they ventured here."

The Highland men drew their claymores,
　And gae a warlike shout,
But Johny's merry men kept the yate,
　Nae ane durst venture out.

The lovers rade the live-lang night,
　And safe gat on their way,
And bonny Baby Livingston
　Has gotten Johny Hay.

"Awa, Glenlion! fy for shame!
　Gae hide ye in some den!
You've lettn your bride be stown frae you,
　For a' your armed men."

HYND HORN

NEAR the King's Court was a young child born,
　With a hey lillelu and a how lo lan;
And his name it was called Young Hynd Horn,
　And the birk and the broom blooms bonnie.

Seven lang years he served the King,
　With a hey lillelu and a how lo lan;
And it's a' for the sake o' his daughter Jean,
　And the birk and the broom blooms bonnie.

The King an angry man was he,
  With a hey lillelu and a how lo lan;
He sent Young Hynd Horn to the sea,
  And the birk and the broom blooms bonnie.

Oh! his Love gave him a gay gold ring,
  With a hey lillelu and a how lo lan;
With three shining diamonds set therein,
  And the birk and the broom blooms bonnie.

"As lang as these diamonds keep their hue,
  With a hey lillelu and a how lo lan,
Ye'll know I am a lover true,
  And the birk and the broom blooms bonnie.

"But when your ring turns pale and wan,
  With a hey lillelu and a how lo lan,
Then I'm in love with another man,
  And the birk and the broom blooms bonnie."

He's gone to the sea and far away,
  With a hey lillelu and a how lo lan;
And he's stayed for seven lang years and a day,
  And the birk and the broom blooms bonnie:

Seven lang years by land and sea,
  With a hey lillelu and a how lo lan;
And he's aften looked how his ring may be,
  And the birk and the broom blooms bonnie.

One day when he looked this ring upon,
  With a hey lillelu and a how lo lan,
The shining diamonds were pale and wan,
  And the birk and the broom blooms bonnie.

He hoisted sails, and hame cam' he,
  With a hey lillelu and a how lo lan;
Hame unto his ain countrie,
  And the birk and the broom blooms bonnie.

He's left the sea and he's come to land,
  With a hey lillelu and a how lo lan;
And the first he met was an auld beggar-man,
  And the birk and the broom blooms bonnie.

"What news, what news, my silly auld man?
  With a hey lillelu and a how lo lan;
For it's seven lang years since I saw this land,
  And the birk and the broom blooms bonnie."

"No news, no news," doth the beggar-man say,
  With a hey lillelu and a how lo lan;
"But our King's ae daughter she's wedded to-day,
  And the birk and the broom blooms bonnie."

"Wilt thou give to me thy begging coat?
  With a hey lillelu and a how lo lan;
And I'll give to thee my scarlet cloak,
  And the birk and the broom blooms bonnie.

"Give me your auld pike-staff, and hat,
  With a hey lillelu and a how lo lan;
And ye sall be right weel paid for that,
  And the birk and the broom blooms bonnie."

The auld beggar-man cast off his coat,
  With a hey lillelu and a how lo lan,
And he's ta'en up the scarlet cloak,
  And the birk and the broom blooms bonnie.

He's gi'en him his auld pike-staff and hat,
  With a hey lillelu and a how lo lan;
And he was right weel paid for that,
  And the birk and the broom blooms bonnie.

The auld beggar-man was bound for the mill,
  With a hey lillelu and a how lo lan;
But Young Hynd Horn for the King's ain hall,
  And the birk and the broom blooms bonnie.

When he came to the King's ain gate,
  With a hey lillelu and a how lo lan,
He asked a drink for Young Hynd Horn's sake,
  And the birk and the broom blooms bonnie.

These news unto the bonny bride cam',
  With a hey lillelu and a how lo lan,
That at the gate there stands an auld man,
  And the birk and the broom blooms bonnie.

There stands an auld man at the King's gate,
With a hey lillelu and a how lo lan;
He asketh a drink for Young Hynd Horn's sake,
And the birk and the broom blooms bonnie.

The Bride cam' tripping down the stair,
With a hey lillelu and a how lo lan;
The combs o' fine goud in her hair,
And the birk and the broom blooms bonnie;

A cup o' the red wine in her hand,
With a hey lillelu and a how lo lan;
And that she gave to the beggar-man,
And the birk and the broom blooms bonnie.

Out o' the cup he drank the wine,
With a hey lillelu and a how lo lan;
And into the cup he dropt the ring,
And the birk and the broom blooms bonnie.

"O gat thou this by sea or by land?
With a hey lillelu and a how lo lan.
Or gat thou it aff a dead man's hand?
And the birk and the broom blooms bonnie."

"I gat it neither by sea nor land,
With a hey lillelu and a how lo lan,
Nor gat I it from a dead man's hand,
And the birk and the broom blooms bonnie.

"But I gat it at my wooing gay,
  With a hey lillelu and a how lo lan;
And I gie it to you on your wedding-day,
  And the birk and the broom blooms bonnie."

"I'll cast aside my satin goun,
  With a hey lillelu and a how lo lan.
And I'll follow you frae toun to toun,
  And the birk and the broom blooms bonnie.

"I'll tak' the fine goud frae my hair,
  With a hey lillelu and a how lo lan,
And follow you forevermair,
  And the birk and the broom blooms bonnie."

He let his cloutie cloak doun fa',
  With a hey lillelu and a how lo lan;
Young Hynd Horn shone above them a',
  And the birk and the broom blooms bonnie,

The bridegroom thought he had her wed,
  With a hey lillelu and a how lo lan;
But she is Young Hynd Horn's instead,
  And the birk and the broom blooms bonnie.
                    Arranged by William Allingham

YOUNG BEICHAN AND SUSIE PYE

PART I

In London was young Beichan born,
    He longed strange countries for to see;
But he was taen by a savage Moor,
    Who handled him right cruellie;

For he viewed the fashions of that land;
    Their way of worship viewed he;
But to Mahound, or Termagant,
    Would Beichan never bend a knee.

So in every shoulder they've putten a bore;
    In every bore they've putten a tree;
And they have made him trail the wine
    And spices on his fair bodie.

They've casten him in a dungeon deep,
    Where he could neither hear nor see;
For seven years they kept him there,
    Till he for hunger's like to die.

This Moor he had but ae daughter,
    Her name was called Susie Pye;
And every day as she took the air,
    Near Beichan's prison she passed by.

O so it fell, upon a day
    She heard young Beichan sadly sing:

My hounds they all go masterless;
My hawks they flee from tree to tree;
My younger brother will heir my land;
Fair England again I'll never see!

All night long no rest she got,
Young Beichan's song for thinking on;
She's stown the keys from her father's head,
And to the prison strong is gone.

And she has opend the prison doors,
I wot she opend two or three,
Ere she could come young Beichan at,
He was locked up so curiouslie.

But when she came young Beichan before,
Sore wonderd he that may to see;
He took her for some fair captive; —
"Fair Lady, I pray, of what countrie?"

"O have ye any lands," she said,
"Or castles in your own countrie,
That ye could give to a lady fair,
From prison strong to set you free?"

"Near London town I have a hall,
With other castles two or three;
I'll give them all to the lady fair
That out of prison will set me free."

"Give me the truth of your right hand,
  The truth of it give unto me,
That for seven years ye'll no lady wed,
  Unless it be along with me."

"I'll give thee the truth of my right hand,
  The truth of it I'll freely gie,
That for seven years I'll stay unwed,
  For the kindness thou dost show to me."

She's gi'en him to eat the good spice-cake,
  She's gi'en him to drink the blood-red wine;
She's bidden him sometimes think on her,
  That sae kindly freed him out of pine.

She's broken a ring from her finger,
  And to Beichan half of it gave she:
"Keep it, to mind you of that love
  The lady bore that set you free.

"And set your foot on good ship-board,
  And haste ye back to your own countrie;
And before that seven years have an end,
  Come back again, love, and marry me."

PART II

But long ere seven years had an end,
  She longd full sore her love to see;
For ever a voice within her breast
  Said, "Beichan has broke his vow to thee."

So she's set her foot on good ship-board,
  And turnd her back on her own countrie.

She sailed east, she sailed west,
  Till to fair England's shore she came;
Where a bonny shepherd she espied,
  Feeding his sheep upon the plain.

"What news, what news, thou bonny shep-
    herd?
What news hast thou to tell to me?"
"Such news I hear, ladie," he says,
  "The like was never in this countrie.

"There is a wedding in yonder hall,
  Has lasted these thirty days and three;
Young Beichan will not wed his bride,
  For love of one that's yond the sea."

She's put her hand in her pocket,
  Gi'en him the gold and white monie;
"Hae, take ye that, my bonny boy,
  For the good news thou tell'st to me."

When she came to young Beichan's gate,
  She tirled softly at the pin;
So ready was the proud porter
  To open and let this lady in.

"Is this young Beichan's hall," she said,
  "Or is that noble lord within?"
"Yea, he's in the hall among them all,
  And this is the day o' his weddin."

"And has he wed anither love?
  And has he clean forgotten me?"
And sighin' said that gay ladie,
  "I wish I were in my own countrie!"

And she has taen her gay gold ring,
  That with her love she break so free;
Says, "Gie him that, ye proud porter,
  And bid the bridegroom speak to me."

When the porter came his lord before,
  He kneeled down low on his knee:
"What aileth thee, my proud porter,
  Thou art so full of courtesie?"

"I've been porter at your gates,
  It's thirty long years now and three;
But there stands a lady at them now,
  The like o' her did I never see;

"For on every finger she has a ring,
  And on her mid-finger she has three,
And as meickle gold aboon her brow
  As would buy an earldom to me."

Its out then spak the bride's mother,
   Aye, and an angry woman was shee;
"Ye might have excepted our bonny bride,
   And twa or three of our companie."

"O hold your tongue, thou bride's mother,
   Of all your folly let me be;
She's ten times fairer nor the bride,
   And all that's in your companie.

"She begs one sheave of your white bread,
   But and a cup of your red wine;
And to remember the lady's love,
   That last reliev'd you out of pine."

"O well-a-day!" said Beichan then,
   "That I so soon have married thee;
For it can be none but Susie Pye,
   That sailed the sea for love of me."

And quickly hied he down the stair;
   Of fifteen steps he made but three;
He's taen his bonny love in his arms,
   And kist and kist her tenderlie.

"O hae ye taen anither bride?
   And hae ye quite forgotten me?
And hae ye quite forgotten her,
   That gave you life and libertie?"

She looked o'er her left shoulder,
  To hide the tears stood in her e'e:
"Now fare thee well, young Beichan," she says,
  "I'll try to think no more on thee."

"O never, never, Susie Pye,
  For surely this can never be;
Nor ever shall I wed but her
  That's done and dree'd so much for me."

Then out and spak the forenoon bride,
  "My lord, your love it changeth soon;
This morning I was made your bride,
  And another chose ere it be noon."

"O hold thy tongue, thou forenoon bride,
  My true love, thou canst never be;
And whan ye return to your own countrie,
  A double dower I'll send with thee."

He's taen Susie Pye by the white hand,
  And gently led her up and down;
And ay as he kist her red rosy lips,
  "Ye're welcome, jewel, to your own."

He's taen her by the milk-white hand,
  And led her to yon fountain stane;
He's changed her name from Susie Pye,
  And he's call'd her his bonny love, Lady Jane.
                              (*Condensed*)

THE CHILD OF ELLE

PART I

On yonder hill a castle stands,
  With walls and towers bedight,
And yonder lives the Child of Elle,
  A young and comely Knight.

The Child of Elle to his garden went,
  And stood at his garden pale,
When, lo! he beheld Fair Emmeline's page
  Come tripping down the dale.

The Child of Elle he hied him thence
  Y-wis he stood not still,
And soon he met Fair Emmeline's page
  Come climbing up the hill.

"Now Christ thee save, thou little foot-
      page!
  Now Christ thee save and see!
Oh! tell me how does thy Lady gay,
  And what may thy tidings be?"

"My Lady, she is all woe-begone,
  And the tears they fall from her eyne;
And aye she laments the deadly feud
  Between her house and thine.

"And here she sends thee a silken scarf,
  Bedewed with many a tear,
And bids thee sometimes think on her,
  Who loved thee so dear.

"And here she sends thee a ring of gold,
  The last boon thou mayst have,
And bids thee wear it for her sake,
  When she is laid in grave.

"For, ah! her gentle heart is broke,
  And in grave soon must she be,
Sith her father hath chose her a new, new love,
  And forbid her to think of thee.

"Her father hath brought her a carlish Knight,
  Sir John of the North Countraye,
And within three days she must him wed,
  Or he vows he will her slay."

"Now, hie thee back, thou little foot-page,
  And greet thy Lady from me,
And tell her that I, her own true love,
  Will die or set her free.

"Now, hie thee back, thou little foot-page,
  And let thy fair Lady know,
This night will I be at her bower-window
  Betide me weal or woe!"

The boy he tripped, the boy he ran,
　　He neither stint nor stayed
Until he came to Fair Emmeline's bower,
　　When kneeling down he said: —

"O Lady, I've been with thy own true love,
　　And he greets thee well by me;
This night will he be at thy bower-window,
　　And die or set thee free."

PART II

Now day was gone, and night was come,
　　And all were fast asleep,
All save the Lady Emmeline,
　　Who sate in her bower to weep:

And soon she heard her true love's voice
　　Low whispering at the wall,
"Awake! awake! my dear Lady,
　　'T is I, thy true love call.

"Awake! awake! my Lady dear,
　　Come, mount this fair palfray;
This ladder of ropes will let thee down,
　　I'll carry thee hence away."

"Now nay, now nay, thou gentle Knight,
　　Now nay, this may not be,
For aye should I tint my maiden fame,
　　If alone I should wend with thee."

"O Lady, thou with a Knight so true,
  Mayst safely wend alone;
To my lady-mother I will thee bring,
  Where marriage shall make us one."

"My father he is a Baron bold,
  Of lineage proud and high;
And what would he say, if his daughter
  Away with a Knight should fly?

"Ah! well I wot, he never would rest,
  Nor his meat should do him no good,
Till he had slain thee, Child of Elle,
  And seen thy dear heart's blood!"

"O Lady, wert thou in thy saddle set,
  And a little space him fro,
I would not care for thy cruel father,
  Nor the worst that he could do.

"O Lady, wert thou in thy saddle set,
  And once without this wall,
I would not care for thy cruel father,
  Nor the worst that might befall."

Fair Emmeline sighed, Fair Emmeline wept,
  And aye her heart was woe:
At length he seized her lily-white hand,
  And down the ladder he drew.

And thrice he clasped her to his breast,
  And kissed her tenderly,
The tears that fell from her fair eyes,
  Ran like the fountain free.

He mounted himself on his steed so tall,
  And her on a fair palfray,
And slung his bugle about his neck,
  And roundly they rode away.

All this beheard her own damsel,
  In her bed whereas she lay,
Quoth she, "My Lord shall know of this,
  So I shall have gold and fee!"

"Awake! awake! thou Baron bold!
  Awake! my noble Dame!
Your daughter is fled with the Child of Elle
  To do the deed of shame!"

The Baron he woke, the Baron he rose,
  And called his merry men all:
"And come thou forth, Sir John the Knight,
  The Lady is carried to thrall!"

PART III

FAIR EMMELINE scant had ridden a mile,
  A mile forth of the town,
When she was aware of her father's men
  Come galloping over the down.

And foremost came the carlish Knight,
  Sir John of the North Countraye,
"Now stop! now stop! thou false traitor,
  Nor carry that Lady away!

"For she is come of high lineage,
  And was of a Lady born,
And ill it beseems thee, a false churl's son,
  To carry her hence to scorn!"

"Now loud thou liest, Sir John the Knight,
  Now thou dost lie of me,
My father's a Knight, a Lady me bore,
  So never did none by thee!

"But light now down, my Lady fair,
  Light down, and hold my steed;
While I and this discourteous Knight
  Do try this arduous deed.

"But light now down, my dear Lady,
  Light down, and hold my horse;
While I and this discourteous Knight
  Do try our valour's force."

Fair Emmeline sighed, Fair Emmeline wept,
  And aye her heart was woe,
While twixt her love and the carlish Knight
  Passed many a baleful blow.

The Child of Elle, he fought so well,
　As his weapon he waved amain,
That soon he had slain the carlish Knight,
　And laid him upon the plain.

And now the Baron and all his men
　Full fast approached nigh:
Ah! what may Lady Emmeline do?
　'T were now no boot to fly!

Her lover, he put his horn to his mouth,
　And blew both loud and shrill,
And soon he saw his own merry men
　Come riding over the hill.

"Now hold thy hand, thou bold Baron,
　I pray thee, hold thy hand,
Nor ruthless rend two gentle hearts
　Fast knit in true love's band.

"Thy daughter I have dearly loved,
　Full long and many a day;
But with such love as holy Kirk
　Hath freely said we may.

"Oh! give consent she may be mine,
　And bless a faithful pair;
My lands and livings are not small,
　My house and lineage fair,

"My mother she was an Earl's daughter,
   And a noble Knight my sire —"
The Baron he frowned, and turned away
   With mickle dole and ire.

Fair Emmeline sighed, Fair Emmeline wept,
   And did all trembling stand;
At length she sprang upon her knee,
   And held his lifted hand.

"Pardon, my Lord and Father dear,
   This fair young Knight and me!
Trust me, but for the carlish Knight,
   I never had fled from thee.

"Oft have you called your Emmeline,
   Your darling and your joy;
Oh! let not then your harsh resolves
   Your Emmeline destroy."

The Baron he stroked his dark-brown cheek,
   And turned his head aside
To wipe away the starting tear,
   He proudly strave to hide.

In deep revolving thought he stood,
   And mused a little space:
Then raised Fair Emmeline from the ground,
   With many a fond embrace.

"Here, take her, Child of Elle," he said
    And gave her lily hand:
"Here, take my dear and only child,
    And with her half my land.

"Thy father once mine honour wronged
    In days of youthful pride;
Do thou the injury repair
    In fondness for thy bride.

"And as thou love her, and hold her dear,
    Heaven prosper thee and thine;
And now my blessing wend wi' thee,
    My lovely Emmeline."

                    Attributed in part to Bishop Percy
                    (*In modern spelling*)

FOR HALLOWEEN AND MIDSUMMER EVE

THE SPELL

At eve last Midsummer, no sleep I sought,
But to the field a bag of Hempseed brought;
I scattered round the seed on every side,
And three times in a trembling accent cried:
"This Hempseed with my virgin hand I sow,
Who shall my True-love be, the crop shall mow!"
I straight looked back, and if my eyes speak truth,
With his keen scythe behind me came the youth!
 With my sharp heel I three times mark the ground,
 And turn me thrice, around, around, around!

Last May-day Fair, I searched to find a Snail,
That might my secret Lover's name reveal.
Two Hazel-nuts I threw into the flame,
And to each nut I gave a sweetheart's name.
This with the loudest bounce me sore amazed,
That in a flame of brightest colour blazed.
 With my sharp heel, I three times mark the ground,
 And turn me thrice, around, around, around!

This mellow Pippin which I pare around,
My Shepherd's name shall flourish on the ground.
I fling the unbroken paring o'er my head,
Upon the grass a perfect L is read.
Yet on my heart a fairer L is seen
Than what the paring marks upon the green.
 With my sharp heel, I three times mark the ground,
 And turn me thrice, around, around, around!
                                    John Gay. (**Condensed**)

THE YOUNG TAMLANE

"O I FORBID ye, maidens a',
   That wear gowd on your hair,
To come or gae by Carterhaugh,
   For young Tamlane is there."

But up then spake her, fair Janet,
   The fairest o' a' her kin;
"I'll cum and gang to Carterhaugh,
   And ask nae leave o' him."

Janet has kilted her green kirtle,
   A little abune her knee;
And she has braided her yellow hair,
   A little abune her bree.

And when she came to Carterhaugh,
   She gaed beside the well;
And there she fand his steed standing,
   But awa was himsell.

She hadna pu'd a red red rose,
   A rose but barely three;
Till up and starts a wee wee man,
   At lady Janet's knee.

Says — "Why pu' ye the rose, Janet?
    What gars ye break the tree?
Or why come ye to Carterhaugh,
    Withouten leave o' me ?" —

Says — "Carterhaugh it is mine ain;
    My daddie gave it me:
I'll come and gang to Carterhaugh,
    And ask nae leave o' thee.

"The truth ye'll tell to me, Tamlane:
    A word ye mauna lie;
Gin e'er ye was in haly chapel,
    Or sained in Christentie?" —

"The truth I'll tell to thee, Janet,
    A word I winna lee:
My father's a knight, a lady me bore,
    As well as they did thee.

"Randolph, earl Murray, was my sire,
    Dunbar, earl March, is thine;
We loved when we were children small,
    Which yet you well may mind.

"When I was a boy just turn'd of nine,
    My uncle sent for me,
To hunt, and hawk, and ride with him,
    And keep him cumpanie.

" There came a wind out of the north,
    A sharp wind and a snell;
And a dead sleep came over me,
    And frae my horse I fell.

"The Queen of Fairies keppit me
    In yon green hill to dwell;
And I'm a fairy, lyth and limb;
    Fair ladye, view me well.

"But we, that live in Fairy-land,
    No sickness know nor pain,
I quit my body when I will,
    And take to it again.

"I quit my body when I please,
    Or unto it repair;
We can inhabit at our ease,
    In either earth or air.

"Our shapes and size we can convert
    To either large or small;
An old nut-shell's the same to us
    As is the lofty hall.

"We sleep in rose-buds soft and sweet,
    We revel in the stream;
We wanton lightly on the wind,
    Or glide on a sunbeam.

"And all our wants are well supplied
From every rich man's store,
Who thankless sins the gifts he gets,
And vainly grasps for more.

"Then I would never tire, Janet,
In Elfish land to dwell;
But aye, at every seven years,
They pay the teind to hell;
And I am sae fat and fair of flesh,
I fear 't will be mysell.

"This night is Hallowe'en, Janet,
The morn is Hallowday;
And, gin ye dare your true love win,
Ye na hae time to stay.

"The night it is good Hallowe'en,
When fairy folk will ride;
And they that wad their true love win
At Miles Cross they maun bide." —

"But how shall I thee ken, Tamlane?
Or how shall I thee knaw,
Amang so many unearthly knights,
The like I never saw?" —

"The first company that passes by,
Say na, and let them gae;

The next company that passes by,
   Say na, and do right sae;
The third company that passes by,
   Then I 'll be ane o' thae.

"First let pass the black, Janet,
   And syne let pass the brown;
But grip ye to the milk-white steed,
   And pu' the rider down.

"For I ride on the milk-white steed,
   And aye nearest the town;
Because I was a christen'd knight,
   They gave me that renown.

"My right hand will be gloved, Janet,
   My left hand will be bare;
And these the tokens I gie thee,
   Nae doubt I will be there.

"They 'll turn me in your arms, Janet,
   An adder and a snake;
But haud me fast, let me not pass,
   Gin ye wad be my maik.

"They 'll turn me in your arms, Janet,
   An adder and an ask;
They 'll turn me in your arms, Janet,
   A bale that burns fast.

"They'll turn me in your arms, Janet,
  A red-hot gad o' airn;
But haud me fast, let me not pass,
  For I'll do you no harm.

"And, next, they'll shape me in your arms,
  A tod, but and an eel;
But haud me fast, nor let me gang,
  As you do love me weel.

"They'll shape me in your arms, Janet,
  A dove, but and a swan;
And, last, they'll shape me in your arms
  A mother-naked man:
Cast your green mantle over me —
  I'll be myself again." —

PART II

GLOOMY, gloomy, was the night,
  And eiry was the way,
As fair Janet in her green mantle,
  To Miles Cross she did gae.

The heavens were black, the night was dark,
  And dreary was the place;
But Janet stood, with eager wish,
  Her lover to embrace.

Betwixt the hours of twelve and one,
  A north wind tore the bent;

And straight she heard strange elritch sounds,
    Upon that wind which went.

About the dead hour o' the night,
    She heard the bridles ring;
And Janet was as glad o' that
    As any earthly thing.

Their oaten pipes blew wondrous shrill,
    The hemlock small blew clear;
And louder notes from hemlock large,
    And bog-reed, struck the ear;
But solemn sounds, or sober thoughts,
    The Fairies cannot bear.

They sing, inspired with love and joy,
    Like skylarks in the air;
Of solid sense, or thought that's grave,
    You'll find no traces there.

Fair Janet stood, with mind unmoved,
    The dreary heath upon;
And louder, louder wax'd the sound,
    As they came riding on.

Will o' Wisp before them went,
    Sent forth a twinkling light;
And soon she saw the fairy bands
    All riding in her sight.

And first gaed by the black, black steed,
    And then gaed by the brown;
But fast she gript the milk-white steed,
    And pu'd the rider down.

She pu'd him frae the milk-white steed,
    And loot the bridle fa';
And up there raise an erlish cry —
    "He's won amang us a'!" —

They shaped him in fair Janet's arms,
    A tod, but and an eel;
She held him fast in every shape —
    As she did love him weel.

They shaped him in her arms at last,
    A mother-naked man;
She wrapt him in her green mantle,
    And sae her true love wan!

Up then spake the queen o' fairies,
    Out o' a bush o' broom —
"She that has borrow'd young Tamlane,
    Has gotten a stately groom." —

Up then spake the queen o' Fairies,
    Out o' a bush o' rye —
"She's ta'en awa the bonniest knight
    In a' my cumpanie.

"But had I kenn'd, Tamlane," she says,
  "A ladye wad borrow'd thee —
I wad ta'en out thy twa grey een,
  Put in twa een o' tree.

"Had I but kenn'd, Tamlane," she says,
  " Before ye came frae hame —
I wad ta'en out your heart o' flesh,
  Put in a heart o' stane.

"Had I but had the wit yestreen
  That I hae coft the day —
I'd paid my kane seven times to hell
  Ere you'd been won away!"

(Condensed)

THE WIFE OF USHER'S WELL

THERE lived a wife at Usher's Well,
  And a wealthy wife was she,
She had three stout and stalwart sons,
  And sent them o'er the sea.

They hadna been a week from her,
  A week but barely ane,
When word came back to the carline wife,
  That her three sons were gane.

They hadna been a week from her,
    A week but barely three,
When word came to the carline wife,
    That her sons she'd never see.

"I wish the wind may never cease,
    Nor fashes in the flood,
Till my three sons come hame to me,
    In earthly flesh and blood!"—

It fell about the Martinmas,
    When nights are lang and mirk,
The carline wife's three sons cam hame,
    And their hats were o' the birk.

It neither grew in syke nor ditch,
    Nor yet in ony sheugh;
But at the gates o' Paradise,
    That birk grew fair eneuch.

  .   .   .   .

"Blow up the fire, my maidens!
    Bring water from the well!
For a' my house shall feast this night,
    Since my three sons are well."—

And she has made to them a bed,
    She's made it large and wide;
And she's ta'en her mantle her about,
    Sat down at the bedside.

  .   .   .   .

Up then crew the red red cock,
　And up and crew the gray;
The eldest to the youngest said,
　"'T is time we were away." —

The cock he hadna craw'd but ance,
　And clapp'd his wings at a',
When the youngest to the eldest said,
　"Brother, we must awa. —

"The cock doth craw, the day doth daw
　The channerin' worm doth chide;
Gin we be mist out o' our place,
　A sair pain we maun bide.

"Fare ye weel, my mother dear!
　Fareweel to barn and byre!
And fare ye weel, the bonny lass,
　That kindles my mother's fire."

SIR ROLAND

WHAN he cam to his ain luve's bouir,
　He tirled at the pin;
And sae ready was his fair fause luve
　To rise and let him in.

"Oh! welcome, welcome, Sir Roland," she says,
　"Thrice welcome thou art to me;

For this night thou wilt feast in my secret
    bouir
And to-morrow we'll wedded be."

"This night is Hallow Eve," he said,
    "And to-morrow is Hallow-day;
And I dreamed a drearie dream yestreen,
    That has made my heart fu' wae.

"I dreamed a drearie dream yestreen,
    And I wish it may come to gude;
I dreamed that ye slew my best grew hound,
    And gied me his lappered blude."

   .   .   .   .

"Unbuckle your belt, Sir Roland," she said,
    "And set you safely down."
"Oh! your chamber is very dark, fair maid,
    And the night is wondrous lown."

"Yes, dark dark is my secret bowir,
    And lown the midnight may be;
For there is none waking in a' this tower
    But thou, my true love, and me."

   .   .   .   .

She has mounted on her true love's steed,
    By the ae light o' the moon;
She has whipped him and spurred him,
    And roundly she rade frae the toun.

She hadna ridden a mile o' gate,
  Never a mile but ane,
Whan she was aware of a tall young man,
  Slow riding o'er the plain.

She turned her to the right about,
  Then to the left turned she;
But aye 'tween her and the wan moonlight.
  That tall Knight did she see.

And he was riding burd alane,
  On a horse as black as jet;
But tho' she followed him fast and fell,
  No nearer could she get.

"Oh stop! Oh stop! young man," she said;
  "For I in dule am dight;
Oh stop, and win a fair lady's luve.
  If you be a leal true Knight."

But nothing did the tall Knight say,
  And nothing did he blin;
Still slowly rode he on before
  And fast she rade behind.

She whipped her steed, she spurred her steed,
  Till his breast was all a foam;
But nearer unto that tall young Knight,
  The Lady, she could not come.

"Oh, if you be a gay young Knight,
　　As well I trow you be,
Pull tight your bridle reins, and stay
　　Till I come up to thee."

But nothing did that tall Knight say,
　　And no whit did he blin,
Until he reached a broad river's side
　　And there he drew his rein.

"Oh, is this water deep?" he said,
　" As it is wondrous dun?
Or is it sic as a saikless maid
　　And a leal true Knight may swim?"

"The water it is deep," she said,
　　"As it is wondrous dun;
But it is sic as a saikless maid
　　And a leal true Knight may swim."

The Knight spurred on his tall black steed;
　　The Lady spurred on her brown;
And fast they rade into the flood,
　　And fast they baith swam down.

"The water weets my tae," she said'
　　"The water weets my knee;
And hold up my bridle reins, Sir Knight,
　　For the sake of Our Ladye."

"If I would help thee now," he said,
  "It were a deadly sin;
For I've sworn neir to trust a fair may's word,
  Till the water weets her chin."

"Oh! the water weets my waist," she said;
  "Sae does it weet my skin;
And my aching heart rins round about,
  The burn maks sic a din.

"The water is waxing deeper still,
  Sae does it wax mair wide;
And aye the farther that we ride on,
  Farther off is the other side.

"Oh, help me now, thou fause fause Knight!
  Have pity on my youth;
For now the water jawes owre my head,
  And it gurgles in my mouth."

The Knight turned right and round about,
  All in the middle stream;
And he stretched out his head to that Ladie
  But loudly she did scream!

"Oh, this is Hallow-morn," he said,
  "And it is your bridal day;
But sad would be that gay wedding,
  If bridegroom and bride were away.

"And ride on, ride on, proud Margaret!
  Till the water comes o'er your bree;
For the bride maun ride deep and deeper yet,
  Wha rides this ford wi' me!

"Turn round, turn round, proud Margaret!
  Turn ye round, and look on me!
Thou hast killed a true Knight under trust,
  And his Ghost now links on with thee."

THE SKELETON IN ARMOUR

"SPEAK! speak! thou fearful guest!
  Who, with thy hollow breast
  Still in rude armour drest,
    Comest to daunt me!
  Wrapt not in Eastern balms,
  But with thy fleshless palms
  Stretched, as if asking alms,
    Why dost thou haunt me?"

Then, from those cavernous eyes
  Pale flashes seemed to rise,
  As when the Northern skies
    Gleam in December;
  And, like the water's flow
  Under December's snow,
  Came a dull voice of woe
    From the heart's chamber.

"I was a Viking old!
  My deeds, though manifold,
  No Skald in song has told,
    No Saga taught thee!
  Take heed, that in thy verse
  Thou dost the tale rehearse,
  Else dread a dead man's curse;
    For this I sought thee.

"Far in the Northern Land,
  By the wild Baltic's strand,
  I, with my childish hand,
    Tamed the gerfalcon;
  And, with my skates fast-bound,
  Skimmed the half-frozen Sound,
  That the poor whimpering hound
    Trembled to walk on.

"Oft to his frozen lair
  Tracked I the grisly bear,
  While from my path the hare
    Fled like a shadow;
  Oft through the forest dark
  Followed the were-wolf's bark,
  Until the soaring lark
    Sang from the meadow.

"But when I older grew,
  Joining a corsair's crew,

O'er the dark sea I flew
   With the marauders.
Wild was the life we led;
Many the souls that sped,
Many the hearts that bled,
   By our stern orders.

"Many a wassail-bout
   Wore the long Winter out;
Often our midnight shout
   Set the cocks crowing,
As we the Berserk's tale
Measured in cups of ale,
Draining the oaken pail,
   Filled to o'erflowing.

"Once as I told in glee
   Tales of the stormy sea,
Soft eyes did gaze on me,
   Burning yet tender;
And as the white stars shine
On the dark Norway pine,
On that dark heart of mine
   Fell their soft splendour.

"I wooed the blue-eyed maid,
   Yielding, yet half afraid,
And in the forest shade
   Our vows were plighted.

Under its loosened vest
Fluttered her little breast,
Like birds within their nest
 By the hawk frighted.

"Bright in her father's hall
Shields gleamed upon the wall,
Loud sang the minstrels all,
 Chanting his glory;
When of old Hildebrand
I asked his daughter's hand,
Mute did the minstrels stand
 To hear my story.

"While the brown ale he quaffed,
Loud then the champion laughed,
And as the wind-gusts waft
 The sea-foam brightly,
So the loud laugh of scorn,
Out of those lips unshorn,
From the deep drinking-horn
 Blew the foam lightly.

"She was a Prince's child,
 I but a Viking wild,
And though she blushed and smiled,
 I was discarded!
Should not the dove so white
Follow the sea-mew's flight,

Why did they leave that night
Her nest unguarded?

"Scarce had I put to sea,
Bearing the maid with me,
Fairest of all was she
    Among the Norsemen!
When on the white sea-strand,
Waving his armed hand,
Saw we old Hildebrand,
    With twenty horsemen.

"Then launched they to the blast,
Bent like a reed each mast,
Yet we were gaining fast,
    When the wind failed us;
And with a sudden flaw
Came round the gusty Skaw,
So that our foe we saw
    Laugh as he hailed us.

"And as to catch the gale
Round veered the flapping sail,
'Death!' was the helmsman's hail,
    'Death without quarter!'
Mid-ships with iron keel
Struck we her ribs of steel;
Down her black hulk did reel
    Through the black water!

"As with his wings aslant,
Sails the fierce cormorant,
Seeking some rocky haunt,
    With his prey laden, —
So toward the open main,
Beating to sea again,
Through the wild hurricane,
    Bore I the maiden.

"Three weeks we westward bore,
And when the storm was o'er,
Cloud-like we saw the shore
    Stretching to leeward;
There for my lady's bower
Built I the lofty tower,
Which, to this very hour,
    Stands looking seaward.

"There lived we many years;
Time dried the maiden's tears;
She had forgot her fears,
    She was a mother;
Death closed her mild blue eyes,
Under that tower she lies;
Ne'er shall the sun arise
    On such another!

"Still grew my bosom then,
Still as a stagnant fen!

Hateful to me were men,
  The sunlight hateful!
In the vast forest here,
Clad in my warlike gear,
Fell I upon my spear,
  Oh, death was grateful!

"Thus, seamed with many scars,
  Bursting these prison bars,
  Up to its native stars
    My soul ascended!
  There from the flowing bowl
  Deep drinks the warrior's soul,
  Skoal! to the Northland! *skoal!*"
    Thus the tale ended.
                    Henry Wadsworth Longfellow

SWEET WILLIAM'S GHOST

THERE came a ghost to Margret's door,
  With many a grievous groan,
And ay he tirled at the pin,
  But answer made she none.

"Is that my father Philip,
  Or is 't my brother John?
Or is 't my true-love, Willy,
  From Scotland new come home?"

" Tis not thy father Philip,
  Nor yet thy brother John;
But tis thy true-love, Willy,
  From Scotland new come home.

"O sweet Margret, O dear Margret,
  I pray thee speak to me;
Give me my faith and troth, Margret,
  As I gave it to thee."

"Thy faith and troth thou's never get,
  Nor yet will I thee lend,
Till that thou come within my bower,
  And kiss my cheek and chin."

"If I shoud come within thy bower,
  I am no earthly man;
And shoud I kiss thy rosy lips,
  Thy days will not be lang.

"O sweet Margret, O dear Margret,
  I pray thee speak to me;
Give me my faith and troth, Margret,
  As I gave it to thee."

"Thy faith and troth thou's never get,
  Nor yet will I thee lend,
Till you take me to yon kirk,
  And wed me with a ring."

"My bones are buried in yon kirk-yard,
  Afar beyond the sea,
And it is but my spirit, Margret,
  That's now speaking to thee."

She stretchd out her lilly-white hand,
  And, for to do her best,
"Hae, there's your faith and troth, Willy,
  God send your soul good rest."

Now she has kilted her robes of green
  A piece below her knee,
And a' the live-lang winter night
  The dead corp followed she.

"Is there any room at your head, Willy?
  Or any room at your feet?
Or any room at your side, Willy,
  Wherein that I may creep?"

"There's no room at my head, Margret,
  There's no room at my feet;
There's no room at my side, Margret,
  My coffin's made so meet."

Then up and crew the red, red cock,
  And up then crew the gray:
"Tis time, tis time, my dear Margret,
  That you were going away."

No more the ghost to Margret said,
  But, with a grievous groan,
Evanishd in a cloud of mist,
  And left her all alone.

"O stay, my only true-love, stay,"
  The constant Margret cry'd;
Wan grew her cheeks, she closd her een,
  Stretchd her soft limbs, and dy'd.

THE EVE OF ST. JOHN

PART I

THE Baron of Smaylho'me rose with day,
  He spurred his courser on,
Without stop or stay, down the rocky way,
  That leads to Brotherstone.

He went not with the bold Buccleuch,
  His banner broad to rear;
He went not 'gainst the English yew,
  To lift the Scottish spear.

Yet his plate-jack was braced, and his helmet
    was laced,
  And his vaunt-brace of proof he wore;
At his saddle-gerthe was a good steel sperthe,
  Full ten pound weight and more.

The Baron returned in three days' space,
 And his looks were sad and sour;
And weary was his courser's pace,
 As he reached his rocky tower.

He came not from where Ancram Moor
 Ran red with English blood;
Where the Douglas true, and the bold Buccleuch,
 'Gainst keen Lord Evers stood.

Yet was his helmet hacked and hewed,
 His acton pierced and tore,
His axe and his dagger with blood imbrued, —
 But it was not English gore.

He lighted at the Chapellage,
 He held him close and still;
And he whistled thrice for his little foot-page,
 His name was English Will.

"Come thou hither, my little foot-page,
 Come hither to my knee;
Though thou art young, and tender of age,
 I think thou art true to me.

"Come, tell me all that thou hast seen,
 And look thou tell me true!
Since I from Smaylho'me tower have been,
 What did thy Lady do?" —

"My Lady, each night, sought the lonely light,
    That burns on the wild Watchfold;
For, from height to height, the beacons bright
    Of the English foemen told.

"The bittern clamoured from the moss,
    The wind blew loud and shrill;
Yet the craggy pathway she did cross,
    To the eiry Beacon Hill.

"I watched her steps, and silent came
    Where she sat her on a stone; —
No watchman stood by the dreary flame,
    It burned all alone.

"The second night I kept her in sight,
    Till to the fire she came,
And, by Mary's might! an armed Knight
    Stood by the lonely flame.

"And many a word that warlike lord
    Did speak to my Lady there;
But the rain fell fast, and loud blew the blast,
    And I heard not what they were.

"The third night there the sky was fair,
    And the mountain blast was still,
As again I watched the secret pair,
    On the lonesome Beacon Hill.

"And I heard her name the midnight hour,
　And name this holy eve;
And say, 'Come this night to thy Lady's bower;
　Ask no bold Baron's leave.

"'He lifts his spear with the bold Buccleuch;
　His Lady is all alone;
The door she'll undo, to her Knight so true,
　On the Eve of good St. John.' —

"'I cannot come; I must not come;
　I dare not come to thee;
On the Eve of St. John I must wander alone:
　In thy bower I may not be.' —

"'Now, out on thee, faint-hearted Knight!
　Thou shouldst not say me nay;
For the eve is sweet, and when lovers meet,
　Is worth the whole summer's day.

"'And I'll chain the bloodhound, and the warder
　　shall not sound,
　And rushes shall be strewed on the stair;
So, by the black rood-stone, and by holy St. John,
　I conjure thee, my Love, to be there!' —

"'Though the bloodhound be mute, and the rush
　　beneath my foot,
　And the warder his bugle should not blow,

Yet there sleepeth a priest in the chamber to the
    East,
  And my footstep he would know.' —

"'O fear not the priest, who sleepeth to the
    East!
For to Dryburgh the way he has ta'en;
And there to say mass, till three days do pass,
  For the soul of a Knight that is slain.' —

"He turned him around, and grimly he frowned;
  Then he laughed right scornfully —
'He who says the mass-rite for the soul of that
    Knight,
  May as well say mass for me:

"'At the lone midnight hour, when bad spirits
    have power,
  In thy chamber will I be.' —
With that he was gone, and my Lady left alone,
  And no more did I see."

Then changed, I trow, was that bold Baron's
    brow,
  From the dark to the blood-red high,
"Now, tell me the mien of the Knight thou hast
    seen,
  For, by Mary, he shall die!" —

"His arms shone full bright, in the beacon's
    red light;
His plume it was scarlet and blue;
On his shield was a hound, in a silver leash
    bound,
    And his crest was a branch of the yew."

"Thou liest, thou liest, thou little foot-page,
    Loud dost thou lie to me!
For that Knight is cold, and low laid in the
    mould,
    All under the Eildon Tree." —

"Yet hear but my word, my noble Lord!
    For I heard her name his name;
And that Lady bright, she called the Knight
    Sir Richard of Coldinghame." —

The bold Baron's brow then changed, I trow,
    From high blood-red to pale —
"The grave is deep and dark — and the corpse
    is stiff and stark —
    So I may not trust thy tale.

"Where fair Tweed flows round holy Melrose,
    And Eildon slopes to the plain,
Full three nights ago, by some secret foe,
    That gay gallant was slain.

"The varying light deceived thy sight,
  And the wild winds drowned the name;
For the Dryburgh bells ring, and the white monks
    do sing,
  For Sir Richard of Coldinghame!"

PART II

HE passed the court-gate, and he oped the tower-
    grate,
  And he mounted the narrow stair,
To the bartizan seat, where, with maids that on
    her wait,
  He found his Lady fair.

That Lady sat in mournful mood;
  Looked over hill and vale;
Over Tweed's fair flood, and Mertoun's wood,
  And all down Teviotdale.

"Now hail, now hail, thou Lady bright!" —
  "Now hail, thou Baron true!
What news, what news, from Ancram fight?
  What news from the bold Buccleuch?" —

"The Ancram Moor is red with gore,
  For many a Southern fell;
And Buccleuch has charged us, evermore,
  To watch our beacons well." —

The Lady blushed red, but nothing she said:
  Nor added the Baron a word:
Then she stepped down the stair to her chamber
    fair,
  And so did her moody lord.

In sleep the Lady mourned, and the Baron tossed
    and turned,
  And oft to himself he said, —
"The worms around him creep, and his bloody
    grave is deep,
  It cannot give up the dead!" —

PART III

It was near the ringing of matin-bell,
  The night was wellnigh done,
When a heavy sleep on that Baron fell,
  On the Eve of good St. John.

The Lady looked through the chamber fair,
  By the light of a dying flame;
And she was aware of a Knight stood there —
  Sir Richard of Coldinghame!

"Alas! away, away!" she cried,
  "For the holy Virgin's sake!" —
"Lady, I know who sleeps by thy side;
  But, Lady, he will not awake.

"By Eildon Tree, for long nights three,
　In bloody grave have I lain;
The mass and the death-prayer are said for me,
　But, Lady, they are said in vain.

"By the Baron's brand, near Tweed's fair strand,
　Most foully slain, I fell;
And my restless sprite on the beacon's height,
　For a space is doomed to dwell.

"At our trysting-place, for a certain space,
　I must wander to and fro;
But I had not had power to come to thy bower,
　Hadst thou not conjured me so." —

Love mastered fear — her brow she crossed;
　"How, Richard, hast thou sped?
And art thou saved, or art thou lost?"
　The vision shook his head!

"Who spilleth life, shall forfeit life;
　So bid thy lord believe:
That lawless love is guilt above,
　This awful sign receive."

He laid his left palm on an oaken beam:
　His right upon her hand;
The Lady shrunk. and fainting sunk,
　For it scorched like a fiery brand.

The sable score, of fingers four,
  Remains on that board impressed;
And for evermore that Lady wore
  A covering on her wrist.

There is a nun in Dryburgh bower,
  Ne'er looks upon the sun;
There is a monk in Melrose tower,
  He speaketh word to none.

That nun, who ne'er beholds the day,
  That monk, who speaks to none —
That nun was Smaylho'me's Lady gay,
  That monk the bold Baron.

                    Sir Walter Scott

ALL UNDER THE GREENWOOD TREE

THE BIRTH O' ROBIN HOOD

And mony ane sings o' grass, o' grass,
And mony ane sings o' corn ;
And mony ane sings o' Robin Hood,
  Kens little whare he was born.

It wasna in the ha', the ha',
  Nor in the painted bower ;
But it was in the gude green wood,
  Amang the lily flower.

ROBIN HOOD AND LITTLE JOHN

WHEN Robin Hood was about twenty years old,
  With a hey down down and a down
He happend to meet Little John,
A jolly brisk blade, right fit for the trade,
  For he was a lusty young man.

Tho he was calld Little, his limbs they were large,
  And his stature was seven foot high;
Where-ever he came, they quak'd at his name,
  For soon he would make them to fly.

How they came acquainted, I'll tell you in brief,
  If you will but listen a while;
For this very jest, amongst all the rest,
  I think it may cause you to smile.

Bold Robin Hood said to his jolly bowmen,
  "Pray tarry you here in this grove;
And see that you all observe well my call,
  While thorough the forest I rove.

"We have had no sport for these fourteen long
      days,
  Therefore now abroad will I go;
Now should I be beat, and cannot retreat,
  My horn I will presently blow.

Then did he shake hands with his merry men all,
  And bid them at present good b'w'ye;
Then, as near a brook his journey he took,
  A stranger he chancd to espy.

They happend to meet on a long narrow bridge,
  And neither of them would give way;
Quoth bold Robin Hood, and sturdily stood,
  "I'll show you right Nottingham play."

With that from his quiver an arrow he drew,
  A broad arrow with a goose-wing:
The stranger reply'd, "I'll liquor thy hide,
  If thou offerst to touch the string."

Quoth bold Robin Hood, ".Thou dost prate like
      an ass,
  For were I to bend but my bow,
I could send a dart quite thro thy proud heart,
  Before thou couldst strike me one blow."

"Thou talkst like a coward," the stranger reply'd;
  "Well armd with a long bow you stand,
To shoot at my breast, while I, I protest,
  Have nought but a staff in my hand."

"The name of a coward," quoth Robin, "I scorn,
  Wherefore my long bow I'll lay by;
And now, for thy sake, a staff will I take,
  The truth of thy manhood to try."

Then Robin Hood stept to a thicket of trees,
  And chose him a staff of ground-oak;
Now this being done, away he did run
  To the stranger, and merrily spoke:

"Lo! see my staff, it is lusty and tough,
  Now here on the bridge we will play;
Whoever falls in, the other shall win
  The battel, and so we'll away."

"With all my whole heart," the stranger reply'd;
  " I scorn in the least to give out;"
This said, they fell to 't without more dispute,
  And their staffs they did flourish about.

And first Robin he gave the stranger a bang,
  So hard that it made his bones ring:
The stranger he said, "This must be repaid,
  I'll give you as good as you bring.

"So long as I'm able to handle my staff,
  To die in your debt, friend, I scorn:"
Then to it each goes, and followd their blows,
  As if they had been threshing of corn.

The stranger gave Robin a crack on the crown,
  Which caused the blood to appear;
Then Robin, enrag'd, more fiercely engag'd,
  And followd his blows more severe.

So thick and so fast did he lay it on him,
   With a passionate fury and ire,
At every stroke, he made him to smoke,
   As if he had been all on fire.

O then into fury the stranger he grew,
   And gave him a damnable look,
And with it a blow that laid him full low,
   And tumbld him into the brook.

"I prithee, good fellow, O where art thou now?"
   The stranger, in laughter, he cry'd;
Quoth bold Robin Hood, "Good faith, in the flood,
   And floating along with the tide.

"I needs must acknowledge thou art a brave soul;
   With thee I'll no longer contend;
For needs must I say, thou hast got the day,
   Our battel shall be at an end."

Then unto the bank he did presently wade,
   And pulld himself out by a thorn;
Which done, at the last, he blowd a loud blast
   Straitway on his fine bugle-horn.

The eccho of which through the vallies did fly,
   At which his stout bowmen appeard,
All cloathed in green, most gay to be seen;
   So up to their master they steerd.

"O what's the matter?" quoth William Stutely;
"Good master, you are wet to the skin:"
"No matter," quoth he; "the lad which you see,
In fighting, hath tumbld me in."

"He shall not go scot-free," the others reply'd;
So strait they were seizing him there,
To duck him likewise; but Robin Hood cries,
"He is a stout fellow, forbear.

"There's no one shall wrong thee, friend, be not
afraid;
These bowmen upon me do wait;
There's threescore and nine; if thou wilt be mine,
Thou shalt have my livery strait.

"And other accoutrements fit for a man;
Speak up, jolly blade, never fear;
I'll teach you also the use of the bow,
To shoot at the fat fallow-deer."

"O here is my hand," the stranger reply'd,
"I'll serve you with all my whole heart;
My name is John Little, a man of good mettle;
Nere doubt me, for I'll play my part."

"His name shall be alterd," quoth William Stutely,
"And I will his godfather be;
Prepare then a feast, and none of the least,
For we will be merry," quoth he.

They presently fetchd in a brace of fat does,
    With humming strong liquor likewise;
They lovd what was good; so, in the greenwood,
    This pretty sweet babe they baptize.

He was, I must tell you, but seven foot high,
    And, may be, an ell in the waste;
A pretty sweet lad; much feasting they had;
    Bold Robin the christning grac'd,

With all his bowmen, which stood in a ring,
    And were of the Nottingham breed;
Brave Stutely comes then, with seven yeomen,
    And did in this manner proceed.

"This infant was called John Little," quoth he,
    "Which name shall be changed anon;
The words we'll transpose, so where-ever he goes,
    His name shall be calld Little John."

They all with a shout made the elements ring,
    So soon as the office was ore;
To feasting they went, with true merriment,
    And tippld strong liquor gillore.

Then Robin he took the pretty sweet babe,
    And cloathd him from top to the toe
In garments of green, most gay to be seen,
    And gave him a curious long bow.

"Thou shalt be an archer as well as the best,
  And range in the greenwood with us;
Where we'll not want gold nor silver, behold,
  While bishops have ought in their purse.

"We live here like squires, or lords of renown,
  Without ere a foot of free land;
We feast on good cheer, with wine, ale, and beer,
  And evry thing at our command."

Then musick and dancing did finish the day;
  At length, when the sun waxed low,
Then all the whole train the grove did refrain,
  And unto their caves they did go.

And so ever after, as long as he livd,
  Altho he was proper and tall,
Yet nevertheless, the truth to express,
  Still Little John they did him call.

ROBIN HOOD AND CLORINDA

WHEN Robin Hood came into merry Sherwood,
  He winded his bugle so clear;
And twice five and twenty good yeomen and bold,
  Before Robin Hood did appear.

"Where are your companions all?" said Robin
    Hood,
  "For still I want forty and three."

Then said a bold yeoman, "Lo, yonder they
    stand,
  All under the green-wood tree."

As that word was spoke, Clorinda came by,
  The queen of the shepherds was she;
And her gown was of velvet as green as the grass,
  And her buskin did reach to her knee.

Her gait it was graceful, her body was straight,
  And her countenance free from pride;
A bow in her hand, and quiver and arrows
  Hung dangling by her sweet side.

Her eye-brows were black, ay, and so was her
    hair,
  And her skin was as smooth as glass;
Her visage spoke wisdom, and modesty too;
  Sets with Robin Hood such a lass!

Said Robin Hood, "Lady fair, whither away?
  O whither, fair lady, away?"
And she made him answer, "To kill a fat buck;
  For to-morrow is Titbury day."

Said Robin Hood, "Lady fair, wander with me
  A little to yonder green bower,
There set down to rest you, and you shall be sure
  Of a brace or a lease, in an hour."

And as we were going towards the green bower,
  Two hundred good bucks we espy'd;
She chose out the fattest that was in the herd,
  And she shot him through side and side.

"By the faith of my body," said bold Robin
    Hood,
  "I never saw woman like thee;
And com'st thou from east, ay, or com'st thou
    from west,
  Thou needst not beg venison of me.

"However, along to my bower you shall go,
  And taste of a forrester's meat:"
And when we come thither we found as good
    cheer
  As any man needs for to eat.

For there was hot venison, and warden pies
    cold,
  Cream clouted, with honey-combs plenty;
And the sarvitors they were, besides Little
    John,
  Good yeomen at least four and twenty.

Clorinda said, "Tell me your name, gentle sir:"
  And he said, "'T is bold Robin Hood:
Squire Gamwel 's my uncle, but all my delight
  Is to dwell in the merry Sherwood;

"For 't is a fine life, and 't is void of all strife."
"So 't is, sir," Clorinda reply'd.
"But oh!" said bold Robin, "how sweet would
    it be,
If Clorinda would be my bride!"

She blusht at the motion; yet, after a pause,
    Said, "Yes, sir, and with all my heart."
"Then let us send for a priest," said Robin
    Hood,
    "And be married before we do part."

When dinner was ended, Sir Roger, the parson
    Of Dubbridge, was sent for in haste:
He brought his mass-book, and he bade them take
    hands,
    And joyn'd them in marriage full fast.

And then, as bold Robin Hood and his sweet
    bride
Went hand in hand to the green bower,
The birds sung with pleasure in merry Sherwood,
    And 't was a most joyful hour.

And when Robin came in the sight of the bower,
    "Where are my yeomen?" said he:
And Little John answer'd, "Lo, yonder they
    stand,
    All under the green-wood tree."

Then a garland they brought her, by two and by
  two,
And plac'd them upon the bride's head:
The music struck up, and we all fell to dance,
  So the bride and bridegroom were wed.
                                   (*Condensed*)

SONG OF THE OUTLAW MURRAY

PART I

ETTRICK FOREST is a fair forest,
  In it grows many a seemly tree;
There's hart and hind, and dae and rae,
  And of a' wild beasts great plentie.

There's a fair Castle, bigged wi' lime and stane;
  O gin it stands not pleasantlie!
In the fore front o' that Castle fair,
  Twa unicorns are bra' to see;
There's the picture of a Knight and a Lady
    bright,
  And the green hollin abune their bree.

There an Outlaw keeps five hundred men,
  He keeps a royal company;
His merrymen a' in ae livery clad,
  O' the Lincoln green sae gay to see;
He and his Lady in purple clad,
  O gin they live not royallie!

Word is gane to our noble King,
  In Edinburgh where that he lay,
That there was an Outlaw in Ettrick Forest,
  Counted him nought, nor a' his courtrie gay.

"I make a vow," then the gude King said,
  "Unto the Man that dear bought me,
I'se either be King of Ettrick Forest,
  Or King of Scotland that Outlaw sall be!"

Then spake the Lord hight Hamilton,
  And to the noble King said he,
"My sovereign Prince, some counsel take,
  First at your nobles, syne at me.

"I rede ye, send yon braw Outlaw till,
  And see gif your man come will he:
Desire him come and be your man,
  And hold of you yon forest free.

"Gif he refuses to do that,
  We'll conquer baith his lands and he!
Or else we'll throw his Castle down,
  And mak' a widow o' his gay Ladye."

The King then called a gentleman,
  James Boyd (the Earl of Arran's brother was
      he);
When James he came before the King,
  He kneeled before him on his knee.

"Welcome, James Boyd!" said our noble King,
  "A message ye maun gang for me;
Ye maun hie to Ettrick Forest,
  To yon Outlaw, where bideth he.

"Ask him of whom he holds his lands,
  Or man wha may his master be,
And desire him come and be my man,
  And hold of me yon forest free.

"To Edinburgh to come and gang,
  His safe warrant I sall gie;
And gif he refuses to do that,
  We'll conquer baith his lands and he.

"Thou mayst vow I'll cast his Castle down,
  And mak' a widow o' his gay Ladye;
I'll hang his merrymen, pair by pair,
  In ony frith where I may them see."

PART II

JAMES BOYD took his leave o' the noble King,
  To Ettrick Forest fair cam' he;
Down Birkendale Brae when that he cam',
  He saw the fair forest wi' his ee.

Baith dae and rae, and hart and hind,
  And of a' wild beasts great plentie;
He heard the bows that boldly ring,
  And arrows whidderan' him near by.

Of that great Castle he got a sight;
  The like he ne'er saw wi' his ee!
On the fore front o' that Castle fair,
  Twa unicorns were bra' to see;
The picture of a Knight, and Lady bright,
  And the green hollin abune their bree.

Thereat he spyed five hundred men,
  Shooting with bows on Newark Lee;
They were a' in ae livery clad,
  O' the Lincoln green sae gay to see.

His men were a' clad in the green,
  The Knight was armed capapie,
With a bended bow, on a milk-white steed;
  And I wot they ranked right bonnilie.

Thereby Boyd kend he was master man,
  And served him in his ain degree.
"God mote thee save, brave Outlaw Murray!
  Thy Ladye, and all thy chivalrie!"
"Marry, thou's welcome, gentleman,
  Some King's messenger thou seems to be."

"The King of Scotland sent me here,
  And, gude Outlaw, I am sent to thee;
I wad wot of whom ye hold your lands,
  Or man wha may thy master be?"

"Thir lands are mine," the Outlaw said;
  "I ken nae King in Christentie;
Frae Soudron I this forest wan,
  When the King nor his Knights were not to
    see."

"He desires you'll come to Edinburgh,
  And hauld of him this forest free;
And, gif ye refuse to do this thing,
  He'll conquer baith thy lands and thee.
He hath vowed to cast thy Castle down,
  And mak' a widow o' thy gay Ladye;

"He'll hang thy merrymen, pair by pair,
  In ony frith where he may them find."
"Ay, by my troth!" the Outlaw said,
  "Than wauld I think me far behind.

"Ere the King my fair country get,
  This land that's nativest to me,
Mony o' his nobles sall be cauld;
  Their ladies sall be right wearie."

Then spak' his Lady, fair of face:
  She said, "'T were without consent of me,
That an outlaw suld come before a King;
  I am right rad of treasonrie.
Bid him be gude to his lords at hame,
  For Edinburgh my Lord sall never see."

PART III

JAMES BOYD took his leave o' the Outlaw keen,
  To Edinburgh boun' is he;
When James he cam' before the King,
  He kneeled lowly on his knee.

"Welcome, James Boyd!" said our noble King,
  "What forest is Ettrick Forest free?"
"Ettrick Forest is the fairest forest
  That ever man saw wi' his ee.

"There's the dae, the rae, the hart, the hind,
  And of a' wild beasts great plentie;
There's a pretty Castle of lime and stane,
  Oh! gin it stands not pleasantlie!

"There's in the fore front o' that Castle
  Twa unicorns, sae bra' to see;
There's the picture of a Knight, and a Lady
      bright
  Wi' the green hollin abune their bree.

"There the Outlaw keeps five hundred men,
  He keeps a royal companie;
His merrymen in ae livery clad,
  O' the Lincoln green sae gay to see:
He and his Lady in purple clad;
  Oh! gin they live right royallie!

"He says, yon forest is his awn;
   He wan it frae the Southronie;
Sae as he wan it, sae will he keep it,
   Contrair all Kings in Christentie."

"Gar warn me Perthshire, and Angus baith,
   Fife, up and down, and Lothians three,
And graith my horse!" said our noble King,
   "For to Ettrick Forest hie will I me."

Then word is gane the Outlaw till,
   In Ettrick Forest, where dwelleth he,
That the King was coming to his countrie,
   To conquer baith his lands and he.

"I mak' a vow," the Outlaw said,
   "I mak' a vow, and that trulie:
Were there but three men to tak' my part,
   Yon King's coming full dear suld be!"

Then messengers he called forth,
   And bade them hie them speedilye:
"Ane of ye gae to Halliday,
   The Laird of the Corehead is he.

"He certain is my sister's son;
   Bid him come quick and succor me;
The King comes on for Ettrick Forest,
   And landless men we a' will be."

"What news? what news?" said Halliday,
  "Man, frae thy master unto me?"
"Not as ye would, seeking your aid;
  The King's his mortal enemie."

"Ay, by my troth!" said Halliday,
  "Even for that it repenteth me;
For gif he lose fair Ettrick Forest,
  He'll tak' fair Moffatdale frae me.

"I'll meet him wi' five hundred men,
  And surely mair, if mae may be;
And before he gets the forest fair,
  We a' will die on Newark Lee!"

The Outlaw called a messenger,
  And bid him hie him speedilye
To Andrew Murray of Cockpool:
  "That man's a dear cousin to me;
Desire him come and mak' me aid
  With a' the power that he may be."

"It stands me hard," Andrew Murray said,
  "Judge gif it stand na hard wi' me;
To enter against a King wi' crown,
  And set my lands in jeopardie!
Yet, if I come not on the day,
  Surely at night he sall me see."

To Sir James Murray of Traquair,
    A message came right speedilye:
"What news? what news?" James Murray said,
    "Man, frae thy master unto me?"

"What needs I tell? for weel ye ken
    The King's his mortal enemie;
And now he is coming to Ettrick Forest,
    And landless men ye a' will be."

"And, by my troth," James Murray said,
    "Wi' that Outlaw will I live and dee;
The King has gifted my lands lang syne, —
    It cannot be nae warse wi' me."

PART IV

The King was coming thro' Caddon Ford,
    And full five thousand men was he;
They saw the dark forest them before,
    They thought it awsome for to see.

Then spak' the Lord hight Hamilton,
    And to the noble King said he,
"My sovereign Liege, some counsel tak',
    First at your nobles, syne at me.

"Desire him meet thee at Permanscore,
    And bring four in his companie;
Five Earls sall gang yoursell before,
    Gude cause that you suld honoured be.

"And, gif he refuses to do that,
　We'll conquer baith his lands and he;
There sall never a Murray, after him,
　Hold land in Ettrick Forest free."

The King then called a gentleman,
　Royal banner-bearer there was he,
James Hoppringle of Torsonse by name;
　He cam' and kneeled upon his knee.

"Welcome, James Pringle of Torsonse!
　A message ye maun gang for me:
Ye maun gae to yon Outlaw Murray,
　Surely where boldly bideth he.

"Bid him meet me at Permanscore,
　And bring four in his companie;
Five Earls sall come wi' mysell,
　Gude reason I suld honoured be.

"And gif he refuses to do that,
　Bid him look for nae good o' me;
There sall never a Murray, after him,
　Have land in Ettrick Forest free."

James cam' before the Outlaw keen,
　And served him in his ain degree:
"Welcome, James Pringle of Torsonse!
　What message frae the King to me?"

"He bids ye meet him at Permanscore,
  And bring four in your company;
Five Earls sall gang himsell before,
  Nae mair in number will he be.

"And gif you refuse to do that,
  (I freely here upgive wi' thee,)
He'll cast yon bonny Castle down,
  And mak' a widow o' that gay Ladye.

"He'll loose yon bloodhound Borderers,
  Wi' fire and sword to follow thee;
There will never a Murray, after thysell,
  Have land in Ettrick Forest free."

"It stands me hard," the Outlaw said,
  "Judge gif it stands na hard wi' me:
What reck o' the losing of mysell,
  But a' my offspring after me!

"Auld Halliday, young Halliday,
  Ye sall be twa to gang wi' me;
Andrew Murray and Sir James Murray,
  We'll be nae mae in companie."

When that they cam' before the King,
  They fell before him on their knee:
"Grant mercy, mercy, noble King!
  E'en for His sake that dyed on tree."

"Sicken like mercy sall ye have,
  On gallows ye sall hangit be!"
"Over God's forbode," quoth the Outlaw then,
  "I hope your Grace will better be!
Else, ere you come to Edinburgh port,
  I trow thin guarded sall ye be.

"Thir lands of Ettrick Forest fair,
  I wan them from the enemie;
Like as I wan them, sae will I keep them,
  Contrair a' Kings in Christentie."

All the nobles the King about,
  Said pity it were to see him dee.
"Yet grant me mercy, sovereign Prince,
  Extend your favour unto me!

"I'll give thee the keys of my Castle,
  Wi' the blessing o' my gay Ladye,
Gin thou'lt make me sheriff of this forest,
  And a' my offspring after me."

"Wilt thou give me the keys of thy Castle,
  Wi' the blessing of thy gay Ladye?
I'se make thee sheriff of Ettrick Forest,
  Surely while upward grows the tree;
If you be not traitor to the King,
  Forfaulted sall thou never be."

"But, Prince, what sall come o' my men?
  When I gae back, traitor they'll ca' me.

I had rather lose my life and land,
  Ere my merrymen rebuked me."

"Will your merrymen amend their lives,
  And a' their pardons I grant thee?
Now, name thy lands where'er they lie,
  And here I render them to thee."

"Fair Philiphaugh is mine by right,
  And Lewinshope still mine shall be;
Newark, Foulshiells, and Tinnies baith,
  My bow and arrow purchased me.

"And I have native steads to me,
  The Newark Lee and Hanginshaw;
I have mony steads in Ettrick Forest,
  But them by name I dinna knaw."

The keys of the Castle he gave the King,
  Wi' the blessing o' his fair Ladye;
He was made sheriff of Ettrick Forest,
  Surely while upward grows the tree;
And if he was na traitor to the King,
  Forfaulted he suld never be.

Wha ever heard, in ony times,
  Sicken an outlaw in his degree
Sic favour get before a King,
  As did Outlaw Murray of the forest free?
        Englished by William Allingham

VALENTINE AND URSINE

PART I

When Flora 'gins to deck the fields
   With colours fresh and fine,
Then holy clerks their matins sing
   To good Saint Valentine!

The King of France that morning fair
   He would a-hunting ride:
To Artois forest prancing forth
   In all his princely pride.

To grace his sports a courtly train
   Of gallant peers attend;
And with their loud and cheerful cries
   The hills and valleys rend.

Through the deep forest swift they pass,
   Through woods and thickets wild;
When down within a lonely dell
   They found a new-born child;

All in a scarlet kercher laid
   Of silk so fine and thin;
A golden mantle wrapt him round,
   Pinned with a silver pin.

The sudden sight surprised them all;
  The courtiers gathered round;
They look, they call, the mother seek;
  No mother could be found.

At length the King himself drew near,
  And as he gazing stands,
The pretty babe looked up and smiled,
  And stretched his little hands.

"Now, by the rood," King Pepin says,
  "This child is passing fair;
I wot he is of gentle blood;
  Perhaps some Prince's heir.

"Go bear him home unto my Court
  With all the care ye may:
Let him be christened Valentine,
  In honour of this day.

"And look me out some cunning nurse;
  Well nurtured let him be;
Nor aught be wanting that becomes
  A bairn of high degree."

They looked him out a cunning nurse,
  And nurtured well was he;
Nor aught was wanting that became
  A bairn of high degree.

PART II

Thus grew the little Valentine,
  Beloved of King and peers;
And showed in all he spake or did
  A wit beyond his years.

But chief in gallant feats of arms
  He did himself advance,
That ere he grew to man's estate
  He had no peer in France.

And now the early down began
  To shade his youthful chin;
When Valentine was dubbed a Knight,
  That he might glory win.

"A boon, a boon, my gracious Liege,
  I beg a boon of thee!
The first adventure that befalls
  May be reserved for me."

"The first adventure shall be thine;"
  The King did smiling say.
Nor many days, when lo! there came
  Three palmers clad in gray.

"Help, gracious Lord," they weeping said;
  And knelt, as it was meet;
"From Artois forest we be come,
  With weak and weary feet.

"Within those deep and dreary woods
   There wends a savage boy;
Whose fierce and mortal rage doth yield
   Thy subjects dire annoy.

"'Mong ruthless bears he sure was bred;
   He lurks within their den:
With bears he lives; with bears he feeds,
   And drinks the blood of men.

"To more than savage strength he joins
   A more than human skill;
For arms, nor cunning may suffice
   His cruel rage to still."

Up then rose Sir Valentine
   And claimed that arduous deed.
"Go forth and conquer," said the King,
   "And great shall be thy meed."

Well mounted on a milk-white steed,
   His armour white as snow;
As well beseemed a virgin Knight,
   Who ne'er had fought a foe,

To Artois forest he repairs
   With all the haste he may;
And soon he spies the savage youth
   A-rending of his prey.

His unkempt hair all matted hung
   His shaggy shoulders round;
His eager eye all fiery glowed;
   His face with fury frowned.

Like eagles' talons grew his nails;
   His limbs were thick and strong;
And dreadful was the knotted oak
   He bare with him along.

Soon as Sir Valentine approached,
   He starts with sudden spring;
And yelling forth a hideous howl,
   He made the forests ring.

As when a tiger fierce and fell
   Hath spied a passing roe,
And leaps at once upon his throat;
   So sprung the savage foe;

So lightly leaped with furious force
   The gentle Knight to seize;
But met his tall uplifted spear,
   Which sunk him on his knees.

A second stroke so stiff and stern
   Had laid the savage low;
But springing up, he raised his club
   And aimed a dreadful blow.

The watchful warrior bent his head,
  And shunned the coming stroke;
Upon his taper spear it fell,
  And all to shivers broke.

Then lighting nimbly from his steed,
  He drew his burnisht brand.
The savage quick as lightning flew
  To wrest it from his hand.

Three times he grasped the silver hilt;
  Three times he felt the blade;
Three times it fell with furious force;
  Three ghastly wounds it made.

Now with redoubled rage he roared;
  His eye-ball flashed with fire;
Each hairy limb with fury shook;
  And all his heart was ire.

Then closing fast with furious gripe
  He clasped the champion round,
And with a strong and sudden twist
  He laid him on the ground.

But soon the Knight, with active spring,
  O'erturned his hairy foe;
And now between their sturdy fists
  Past many a bruising blow.

They rolled and grappled on the ground,
　And there they struggled long:
Skillful and active was the Knight;
　The savage he was strong.

But brutal force and savage strength
　To art and skill must yield:
Sir Valentine at length prevailed,
　And won the well-fought field.

Then binding straight his conquered foe
　Fast with an iron chain,
He ties him to his horse's tail,
　And leads him o'er the plain.

To Court his hairy captive soon
　Sir Valentine doth bring;
And kneeling down upon his knee,
　Presents him to the King.

With loss of blood and loss of strength
　The savage tamer grew;
And to Sir Valentine became
　A servant, tried and true.

And 'cause with bears he erst was bred,
　Ursine they call his name;
A name which unto future times
　The Muses shall proclaim.

PART III

In high renown with Prince and peer
　Now lived Sir Valentine;
His high renown with Prince and peer
　Made envious hearts repine.

It chanced the King upon a day
　Prepared a sumptuous feast;
And there came lords and dainty dames,
　And many a noble guest.

Amid their cups that freely flowed,
　Their revelry and mirth,
A youthful Knight taxed Valentine
　Of base and doubtful birth.

The foul reproach, so grossly urged,
　His generous heart did wound;
And strait he vowed he ne'er would rest
　Till he his parents found.

Then bidding King and peers adieu,
　Early one summer's day,
With faithful Ursine by his side,
　From Court he took his way.

O'er hill and valley, moss and moor,
　For many a day they pass;
At length, upon a moated lake,
　They found a bridge of brass.

Beyond it rose a Castle fair,
　Y-built of marble-stone;
The battlements were gilt with gold,
　And glittered in the sun.

Beneath the bridge, with strange device,
　A hundred bells were hung;
That man, nor beast, might pass thereon
　But strait their larum rung.

This quickly found the youthful pair,
　Who boldly crossing o'er,
The jangling sound bedeafed their ears,
　And rung from shore to shore.

Quick at the sound the castle-gates
　Unlocked and opened wide,
And strait a Giant huge and grim
　Stalked forth with stately pride.

"Now yield you, caitiffs, to my will!"
　He cried with hideous roar;
"Or else the wolves shall eat your flesh,
　And ravens drink your gore."

"Vain boaster," said the youthful Knight,
　"I scorn thy threats and thee;
I trust to force thy brazen gates,
　And set thy captives free."

Then putting spurs unto his steed,
 He aimed a dreadful thrust;
The spear against the Giant glanced
 And caused the blood to burst.

Mad and outrageous with the pain,
 He whirled his mace of steel;
The very wind of such a blow
 Had made the champion reel.

It haply missed; and now the Knight
 His glittering sword displayed,
And riding round with whirlwind speed
 Oft made him feel the blade.

As when a large and monstrous oak
 Unceasing axes hew,
So fast around the Giant's limbs
 The blows quick-darting flew.

As when the boughs with hideous fall
 Some hapless woodman crush,
With such a force the enormous foe
 Did on the champion rush.

A fearful blow, alas! there came;
 Both horse and Knight it took,
And laid them senseless in the dust;
 So fatal was the stroke.

Then smiling forth a hideous grin,
  The Giant strides in haste,
And, stooping, aims a second stroke:
  "Now caitiff breathe thy last!"

But ere it fell, two thundering blows
  Upon his skull descend;
From Ursine's knotty club they came,
  Who ran to save his friend.

Down sunk the Giant gaping wide,
  And rolling his grim eyes;
The hairy youth repeats his blows;
  He gasps, he groans, he dies.

PART IV

QUICKLY Sir Valentine revived
  With Ursine's timely care;
And now to search the castle walls
  The venturous youths repair.

The blood and bones of murdered Knights
  They found where'er they came;
At length within a lonely cell
  They saw a mournful dame.

Her gentle eyes were dimmed with tears;
  Her cheeks were pale with woe;
And long Sir Valentine besought
  Her doleful tale to know.

"Alas! young Knight," she weeping said,
  "Condole my wretched fate;
A childless mother here you see;
  A wife without a mate.

"These twenty winters here forlorn
  I've drawn my hated breath;
Sole witness of a monster's crimes,
  And wishing aye for death.

"Know, I am sister of a King,
  And in my early years
Was married to a mighty Prince,
  The fairest of his peers.

"With him I sweetly lived in love
  A twelvemonth and a day;
When, lo! a foul and treacherous priest
  Y-wrought our loves' decay.

"With treason, villainy, and wrong,
  My goodness he repayed;
With jealous doubts he filled my Lord,
  And me to woe betrayed;

"But, 'cause I then was ill, my Lord
  At length my life he spared;
But bade me instant quit the realm,
  One trusty Knight my guard.

"Forth on my journey I depart,
 Oppressed with grief and woe,
And tow'rds my brother's distant Court,
 With breaking heart, I go.

"Long time thro' sundry foreign lands
 We slowly pace forlorn,
At length within a forest wild,
 I had two babies born.

"The eldest fair and smooth, as snow
 That tips the mountain hoar;
The younger's little body rough
 With hairs was covered o'er.

"But here afresh begin my woes:
 While tender care I took
To shield my eldest from the cold,
 And wrap him in my cloak,

"A prowling bear burst from the wood,
 And seized my younger son;
Affection lent my weakness wings
 And after them I run.

"But all forewearied, weak and spent,
 I quickly swooned away;
And there beneath the greenwood shade
 Long time I lifeless lay.

"At length the Knight brought me relief,
    And raised me from the ground;
But neither of my pretty babes
    Could ever more be found.

"And, while in search we wandered far,
    We met that Giant grim,
Who ruthless slew my trusty Knight,
    And bare me off with him.

"But charmed by Heaven, or else my griefs,
    He offered me no wrong;
Save that within these lonely walls
    I've been immured so long."

"Now, surely," said the youthful Knight,
    "You are Lady Bellisance,
Wife to the Grecian Emperor;
    Your brother's King of France.

"For in your royal brother's Court
    Myself my breeding had;
Where oft the story of your woes
    Hath made my bosom sad.

"If so, know your accuser's dead,
    And dying owned his crime;
And long your Lord hath sought you out
    Thro' every foreign clime.

"And when no tidings he could learn
　Of his much-wronged wife,
He vowed thenceforth within his Court
　To lead a hermit's life."

"Now Heaven is kind!" the Lady said;
　And dropt a joyful tear;
"Shall I once more behold my Lord?
　That Lord I love so dear?"

"But, Madam," said Sir Valentine,
　And knelt upon his knee;
"Know you the cloak that wrapt your babe,
　If you the same should see?"

And pulling forth the cloth of gold
　In which himself was found,
The Lady gave a sudden shriek,
　And fainted on the ground.

But by his pious care revived,
　His tale she heard anon;
And soon by other tokens found
　He was indeed her son.

"But who's this hairy youth?" she said;
　"He much resembles thee;
The bear devoured my younger son,
　Or sure that son were he."

"Madam, this youth with bears was bred,
   And reared within their den.
But recollect ye any mark
   To know your son again?"

"Upon his little side," quoth she,
   "Was stamped a bloody rose."
"Here, Lady, see the crimson mark
   Upon his body grows!"

Then clasping both her new-found sons,
   She bathed their cheeks with tears;
And soon towards her brother's Court
   Her joyful course she steers.

What pen can paint King Pepin's joy,
   His sister thus restored!
And soon a messenger was sent
   To cheer her drooping Lord,

Who came in haste with all his peers,
   To fetch her home to Greece;
Where many happy years they reigned
   In perfect love and peace.

To them Sir Ursine did succeed,
   And long the sceptre bare.
Sir Valentine he stayed in France,
   And was his uncle's heir.

                    Attributed in part to Bishop Percy
                    (*Done into modern spelling*)

O' PILGRIMAGE AND SOULS SO STRONG

THE PILGRIM

What Danger is the Pilgrim in?
  How many are his Foes?
How many ways there are to Sin,
  No living Mortal knows.

Some of the Ditch shy are, yet can
  Lie tumbling on the Myre,
Some, tho' they shun the Frying-Pan,
  Do leap into the Fire.

                              John Bunyan

THE HEART OF THE BRUCE

PART I

THE good Lord Douglas paced the deck,
  And oh, his face was wan!
Unlike the flush it used to wear
  When in the battle-van. —

"Come hither, come hither, my trusty Knight,
  Sir Simon of the Lee;
There is a freit lies near my soul
  I fain would tell to thee.

"Thou know'st the words King Robert spoke
  Upon his dying day:
How he bade me take his noble Heart
  And carry it far away;

"And lay it in the holy soil
  Where once the Saviour trod,
Since he might not bear the blessed Cross,
  Nor strike one blow for God.

"Last night as in my bed I lay,
  I dreamed a dreary dream: —
Methought I saw a Pilgrim stand
  In the moonlight's quivering beam.

"His robe was of the azure dye,
　　Snow-white his scattered hairs,
And even such a cross he bore
　　As good Saint Andrew bears.

"'Why go ye forth, Lord James,' he said,
　　'With spear and belted brand?
Why do you take its dearest pledge
　　From this our Scottish land?

"'The sultry breeze of Galilee
　　Creeps through its groves of palm,
The olives on the Holy Mount
　　Stand glittering in the calm.

"'But 't is not there that Scotland's Heart
　　Shall rest by God's decree,
Till the great Angel calls the dead
　　To rise from earth and sea!

"'Lord James of Douglas, mark my rede!
　　That Heart shall pass once more
In fiery fight against the foe,
　　As it was wont of yore.

"'And it shall pass beneath the Cross,
　　And save King Robert's vow;
But other hands shall bear it back,
　　Not, James of Douglas, thou!'

"Now, by thy knightly faith, I pray,
  Sir Simon of the Lee —
For truer friend had never man
  Than thou hast been to me —

"If ne'er upon the Holy Land
  'T is mine in life to tread,
Bear thou to Scotland's kindly earth
  The relics of her dead."

The tear was in Sir Simon's eye
  As he wrung the warrior's hand —
"Betide me weal, betide me woe,
  I'll hold by thy command.

"But if in battle-front, Lord James,
  'T is ours once more to ride,
Nor force of man, nor craft of fiend,
  Shall cleave me from thy side!"

PART II

AND aye we sailed and aye we sailed,
  Across the weary sea,
Until one morn the coast of Spain
  Rose grimly on our lee.

And as we rounded to the port,
  Beneath the watch-tower's wall,
We heard the clash of the atabals,
  And the trumpet's wavering call.

"Why sounds yon Eastern music here
  So wantonly and long,
And whose the crowd of armed men
  That round yon standard throng?"

"The Moors have come from Africa
  To spoil and waste and slay,
And King Alonzo of Castile
  Must fight with them to-day."

"Now shame it were," cried good Lord James,
  "Shall never be said of me,
That I and mine have turned aside
  From the Cross in jeopardie!

"Have down, have down, my merrymen all —
  Have down unto the plain;
We'll let the Scottish lion loose
  Within the fields of Spain!"

"Now welcome to me, noble Lord,
  Thou and thy stalwart power;
Dear is the sight of a Christian Knight,
  Who comes in such an hour!

"Is it for bond or faith you come,
  Or yet for golden fee?
Or bring ye France's lilies here,
  Or the flower of Burgundie?"

"God greet thee well, thou valiant King,
    Thee and thy belted peers —
Sir James of Douglas am I called,
    And these are Scottish spears.

"We do not fight for bond or plight,
    Nor yet for golden fee;
But for the sake of our blessed Lord,
    Who died upon the tree.

"We bring our great King Robert's Heart
    Across the weltering wave,
To lay it in the holy soil
    Hard by the Saviour's grave.

"True Pilgrims we, by land or sea,
    Where danger bars the way;
And therefore are we here, Lord King,
    To ride with thee this day!"

The King has bent his stately head,
    And the tears were in his eyne —
"God's blessing on thee, noble Knight,
    For this brave thought of thine!

"I know thy name full well, Lord James;
    And honoured may I be,
That those who fought beside the Bruce
    Should fight this day for me!

"Take thou the leading of the van,
  And charge the Moors amain;
There is not such a lance as thine
  In all the host of Spain!"

The Douglas turned towards us then,
  Oh, but his glance was high! —
"There is not one of all my men
  But is as bold as I.

"There is not one of all my Knights
  But bears as true a spear —
Then onwards, Scottish gentlemen,
  And think King Robert 's here!"

PART III

THE trumpets blew, the cross-bolts flew,
  The arrows flashed like flame,
As spur in side, and spear in rest,
  Against the foe we came.

And many a bearded Saracen
  Went down, both horse and man;
For through their ranks we rode like corn,
  So furiously we ran!

But in behind our path they closed,
  Though fain to let us through,
For they were forty thousand men,
  And we were wondrous few.

We might not see a lance's length,
   So dense was their array,
But the long fell sweep of the Scottish blade
   Still held them hard at bay.

"Make in! make in!" Lord Douglas cried —
   "Make in, my brethren dear!
Sir William of Saint Clair is down;
   We may not leave him here!"

But thicker, thicker grew the swarm,
   And sharper shot the rain,
And the horses reared amid the press,
   But they would not charge again.

"Now Jesu help thee," said Lord James,
   "Thou kind and true Saint Clair!
An' if I may not bring thee off,
   I'll die beside thee there!"

Then in his stirrups up he stood,
   So lionlike and bold,
And held the precious Heart aloft
   All in its case of gold.

He flung it from him, far ahead,
   And never spake he more,
But — "Pass thee first, thou dauntless Heart,
   As thou wert wont of yore!"

The roar of fight rose fiercer yet,
  And heavier still the stour,
Till the spears of Spain came shivering in,
  And swept away the Moor.

"Now praised be God, the day is won!
  They fly o'er flood and fell —
Why dost thou draw the rein so hard,
  Good Knight, that fought so well?"

"Oh, ride ye on, Lord King!" he said,
  "And leave the dead to me,
For I must keep the dreariest watch
  That ever I shall dree!

"There lies, above his master's Heart,
  The Douglas, stark and grim;
And woe is me I should be here,
  Not side by side with him!"

The King he lighted from his horse,
  He flung his brand away,
And took the Douglas by the hand,
  So stately as he lay.

"God give thee rest, thou valiant soul!
  That fought so well for Spain;
I'd rather half my land were gone,
  So thou wert here again!"

We bore the good Lord James away,
  And the priceless Heart we bore,
And heavily we steered our ship
  Towards the Scottish shore.

No welcome greeted our return,
  Nor clang of martial tread,
But all were dumb and hushed as death
  Before the mighty dead.

We laid our chief in Douglas Kirk,
  The Heart in fair Melrose;
And woeful men were we that day —
  God grant their souls repose!
      William Edmondstoune Aytoun. (Condensed)

BARCLAY OF URY

Up the streets of Aberdeen,
By the kirk and college green,
  Rode the Laird of Ury;
Close behind him, close beside,
Foul of mouth and evil-eyed,
  Pressed the mob in fury.

Flouted him the drunken churl,
Jeered at him the serving-girl,
  Prompt to please her master;

And the begging carlin, late
Fed and clothed at Ury's gate,
  Cursed him as he passed her.

Yet, with calm and stately mien,
Up the streets of Aberdeen
  Came he slowly riding;
And, to all he saw and heard,
Answering not with bitter word,
  Turning not for chiding.

Came a troop with broadswords swinging,
Bits and bridles sharply ringing,
  Loose and free and froward;
Quoth the foremost, "Ride him down!
Push him! prick him! through the town
  Drive the Quaker coward!"

But from out the thickening crowd
Cried a sudden voice and loud;
  "Barclay! Ho! a Barclay!"
And the old man at his side
Saw a comrade, battle-tried,
  Scarred and sunburned darkly,

Who with ready weapon bare,
Fronting to the troopers there,
  Cried aloud: "God save us!

Call ye coward him who stood
Ankle deep in Lützen's blood,
  With the brave Gustavus?"

"Nay, I do not need thy sword,
Comrade mine," said Ury's lord;
  "Put it up, I pray thee:
Passive to His holy will,
Trust I in my Master still,
  Even though He slay me.

"Pledges of thy love and faith,
Proved on many a field of death,
  Not by me are needed."
Marvelled much that henchman bold,
That his Laird, so stout of old,
  Now so meekly pleaded.

"Woe's the day!" he sadly said,
With a slowly shaking head,
  And a look of pity;
"Ury's honest lord reviled,
Mock of knave and sport of child,
  In his own good city!

"Speak the word, and, master mine,
As we charged on Tilly's line,
  And his Walloon lancers,

Smiting thro' their midst we 'll teach
Civil look and decent speech
   To these boyish prancers!"

"Marvel not, mine ancient friend,
Like beginning, like the end,"
   Quoth the Laird of Ury;
"Is the sinful servant more
Than his gracious Lord who bore
   Bonds and stripes in Jewry?

"Give me joy that in His name,
I can bear, with patient frame,
   All these vain ones offer;
While for them He suffereth long,
Shall I answer wrong with wrong,
   Scoffing with the scoffer?

"Happier I, with loss of all,
Hunted, outlawed, held in thrall,
   With few friends to greet me,
Than when reeve and squire were seen,
Riding out from Aberdeen,
   With bared heads to meet me.

"When each goodwife, o'er and o'er,
Blessed me as I passed her door;
   And the snooded daughter,

Through her casement glancing down,
Smiled on him who bore renown
    From red fields of slaughter.

"Hard to feel the stranger's scoff,
Hard the old friend's falling off,
    Hard to learn forgiving;
But the Lord His own rewards,
And His love with theirs accords,
    Warm and fresh and living.

"Through this dark and stormy night
Faith beholds a feeble light,
    Up the blackness streaking;
Knowing God's own time is best,
In a patient hope I rest
    For the full day-breaking!"

So the Laird of Ury said,
Turning slow his horse's head,
    Towards the Tolbooth prison,
Where through iron gates he heard
Poor disciples of the Word
    Preach of Christ arisen!

Not in vain, Confessor old,
Unto us the tale is told
    Of thy day of trial;

Every age on him who strays
From its broad and beaten ways
  Pours its seven-fold vial.

Happy he whose inward ear
Angel comfortings can hear,
  O'er the rabble's laughter;
And while Hatred's fagots burn,
Glimpses through the smoke discern
  Of the good hereafter.

Knowing this, that never yet
Share of Truth was vainly set
  In the world's wide fallow;
After hands shall sow the seed,
After hands from hill and mead
  Reap the harvests yellow.

Thus, with somewhat of the Seer,
Must the moral pioneer
  From the future borrow;
Clothe the waste with dreams of grain,
And, on midnight's sky of rain,
  Paint the golden morrow!

John Greenleaf Whittier

THE TOUCHSTONE

A MAN there came, whence none could tell,
Bearing a Touchstone in his hand,
And testing all things in the land
By its unerring spell.

A thousand transformations rose
From fair to foul, from foul to fair;
The golden crown he did not spare,
Nor scorn the beggar's clothes.

Of heirloom jewels, prized so much,
Were many changed to chips and clods;
And even statues of the gods
Crumbled beneath its touch.

Then angrily the people cried,
"The loss outweighs the profit far;
Our goods suffice us as they are:
We will not have them tried."

And, since they could not so avail
To check his unrelenting quest,
They seized him, saying, "Let him test
How real is our jail!"

But though they slew him with the sword,
And in a fire his Touchstone burned,

Its doings could not be o'erturned,
Its undoings restored.

And when to stop all future harm,
They strewed its ashes on the breeze,
They little guessed each grain of these,
Conveyed the perfect charm.
William Allingham

SIR GALAHAD

(The Quest of the Holy Grail)

My good blade carves the casques of men,
  My tough lance thrusteth sure,
My strength is as the strength of ten,
  Because my heart is pure.
The shattering trumpet shrilleth high,
  The hard brands shiver on the steel,
The splintered spear-shafts crack and fly,
  The horse and rider reel;
They reel, they roll in clanging lists,
  And when the tide of combat stands,
Perfume and flowers fall in showers,
  That lightly rain from ladies' hands.

How sweet are looks that ladies bend
  On whom their favours fall!
For them I battle till the end,
  To save from shame and thrall;

But all my heart is drawn above,
  My knees are bowed in crypt and shrine,
I never felt the kiss of love,
  Nor maiden's hand in mine.
More bounteous aspects on me beam,
  Me mightier transports move and thrill;
So keep I fair thro' faith and prayer,
  A virgin heart in work and will.

When down the stormy crescent goes,
  A light before me swims,
Between dark stems the forest glows,
  I hear a noise of hymns.
Then by some secret shrine I ride;
  I hear a voice, but none are there;
The stalls are void, the doors are wide,
  The tapers burning fair.
Fair gleams the snowy altar-cloth,
  The silver vessels sparkle clean,
The shrill bell rings, the censer swings,
  And solemn chaunts resound between.

Sometimes on lonely mountain-meres
  I find a magic bark.
I leap on board; no helmsman steers;
  I float till all is dark.
A gentle sound, an awful light!
  Three Angels bear the Holy Grail;
With folded feet, in stoles of white,
  On sleeping wings they sail.

Ah, blessed vision! blood of God!
  My spirit beats her mortal bars,
As down dark tides, the glory slides,
  And starlike mingles with the stars.

When on my goodly charger borne
  Thro' dreaming towns I go,
The cock crows ere the Christmas morn,
  The streets are dumb with snow.
The tempest crackles on the leads,
  And, ringing, springs from brand and mail;
But o'er the dark a glory spreads,
  And gilds the driving hail.
I leave the plain, I climb the height;
  No branchy thicket shelter yields;
But blessed forms in whistling storms
  Fly o'er waste fens and windy fields.

A maiden Knight — to me is given
  Such hope, I know not fear;
I yearn to breathe the airs of Heaven
  That often meet me here.
I muse on joy that will not cease,
  Pure spaces clothed in living beams,
Pure lilies of eternal peace,
  Whose odours haunt my dreams;
And, stricken by an Angel's hand,
  This mortal armour that I wear,
This weight and size, this heart and eyes,
  Are touched, are turned to finest air.

The clouds are broken in the sky,
  And thro' the mountain-walls
A rolling organ-harmony
  Swells up and shakes and falls.
Then move the trees, the copses nod,
  Wings flutter, voices hover clear;
"O just and faithful Knight of God!
  Ride on! the prize is near."
So pass I hostel, hall, and grange;
  By bridge and ford, by park and pale,
All-armed I ride, whate'er betide,
  Until I find the Holy Grail.
                    Alfred, Lord Tennyson

PILGRIMAGE

GIVE me my Scallop-shell of Quiet,
My Staff of Faith to walk upon;
My Scrip of Joy, immortal diet;
My Bottle of Salvation.
My Gown of Glory, (Hope's true Gage)
And thus I'll take my Pilgrimage.

Blood must be my Bodie's only Balmer,
Whilst my Soul like a quiet Palmer,
Travelleth towards the Land of Heaven,
No other Balm will there be given.

Over the Silver Mountains,
Where spring the Nectar Fountains,

There will I kiss the Bowl of Bliss,
And drink mine everlasting fill
Upon every milken Hill.
My Soul will be a-dry before,
But after, it will thirst no more.
I'll take them first, to quench my Thirst,
   And taste of Nectar's Suckets,
      At those clear Wells
      Where Sweetness dwells,
Drawn up by Saints in crystal buckets.

More peaceful Pilgrims I shall see,
That have cast off their Rags of Clay,
And walk apparelled fresh like me,
And when our Bodies and all we
Are filled with Immortality,
Then the blessed Parts we'll travel,
Strowed with Rubies thick as Gravel,
Ceilings of Diamonds, Saphire Flowers,
High Walls of Coral, and pearly Bowers.

From thence to Heaven's bribeless Hall,
Where no corrupted Voices brawl,
No Cause deferred, no vain spent Journey,
For there *Christ* is the King's Attorney,
Who pleads for all without Degrees,
And He hath Angels, but no Fees.

• · •   •   ·   •   · •· • · •

And this is mine eternal Plea,
To Him that made Heaven, Earth and Sea,
That since my Flesh must die so soon,
And want a Head to dine next Noon,
Just at the Stroke, when my Veins start and
      spread,
Set on my Soul an everlasting Head.
Then am I ready, like a Palmer fit,
To tread those blest Paths which before I
      writ.

                 Sir Walter Raleigh. (Condensed)

THE ROYAL COURT

In Royal Courts my Soul hath slept,
   On royal meats I've fed;
Royal favour sheltered me,
   My Soul was wellnigh dead.

The royal eye's now turned away,
   And scorn and dearth are mine;
False-hearted friends are fled afar,
   My Soul awakes to pine.

"Oh! where, my Soul, seek refuge now,
   While mocking foes pursue?
Oh! whither shall I flee away,
   Thou Soul so full of rue?"

"Turn, turn unto this greenwood shade,
    And rest beneath His Tree,
With little birds on every bough
    To sing His peace to thee.

"A loyal King doth here abide,
    Here is his Royal Court;
His carpet green's enamelled bright
    With flowers of every sort.

"His subjects, all the wildwood things,
    He feedeth from His hand;
His messengers are birds and winds,
    His will they understand.

"His table is bedecked with moss;
    His almoners are bees,
The berry-vine, the leaping stream,
    And all the fruitful trees.

"Here shalt thou find a Royal Court
    Where flatt'ry holds no sway;
And gentle is the royal eye,
    Here friendship comes to stay.

"Turn, turn unto the sweet greenwood,
    O happy One! and sing
Praise with the birds and all good life,
    To Christ who is our King!"

Modern, anon.

TRUE VALOUR

Who would true Valour see,
Let him come hither;
One here will constant be,
Come Wind, come Weather.
There's no Discouragement,
Shall make him once Relent,
His first avow'd Intent,
To be a Pilgrim.

Who so beset him round,
With dismal Storys,
Do but themselves confound;
His Strength the more is.
No Lyon *can him fright,*
He'l with a Gyant *Fight,*
But he will have a right,
To be a Pilgrim.

Hobgoblin, *nor foul* Fiend,
Can daunt *his Spirit:*
He knows, he at the end,
Shall Life Inherit.
Then Fancies fly away,
He'l fear not what men say,
He'l *labor Night and Day,*
To be a Pilgrim.

John Bunyan (from reprint of first edition)

PEACE

SWEET Peace, where dost thou dwell, I humbly
    crave?
  Let me once know.
  I sought thee in a secret cave,
  And asked if Peace were there.
A hollow wind did seem to answer, "No!
  Go seek elsewhere."

I did; and going did a Rainbow note:
  "Surely," thought I,
  "This is the lace of Peace's coat;
  I will search out the matter."
But while I looked the clouds immediately
  Did break and scatter.

Then went I to a garden, and did spy
  A gallant flower, —
  The Crown-Imperial. "Sure," said I,
  "Peace at the root must dwell."
But when I digged, I saw a worm devour
  What showed so well.

At length I met a rev'rend, good, old man;
  Whom, when for Peace
  I did demand, he thus began:
  "There was a Prince of old
At Salem dwelt, Who lived with good increase
  Of flock and fold.

"He sweetly lived; yet sweetness did not save
  His life from foes.
  But after death, out of His grave
  There sprang twelve stalks of Wheat;
Which many wondering at got some of those
  To plant and set.

"It prospered strangely, and did soon disperse
  Through all the Earth;
  For they that taste it do rehearse
  That virtue lies therein, —
A secret virtue, bringing Peace and Mirth
  By flight of Sin.

"Take of this grain, which in my garden grows,
  And grows for you:
  Make bread of it; and that repose
  And Peace, which ev'ry where
With so much earnestness you do pursue,
  Is only there."

George Herbert

THE THREE KINGS

THREE Kings came riding from far away,
  Melchior and Gaspar and Baltasar;
Three Wise Men out of the East were they,
And they travelled by night and they slept by day,
  For their guide was a beautiful, wonderful Star.

The Star was so beautiful, large, and clear,
　　That all the other stars of the sky,
Became a white mist in the atmosphere,
And by this they knew that the coming was near
　　Of the Prince foretold in the prophecy.

Three caskets they bore on their saddle-bows,
　　Three caskets of gold with golden keys;
Their robes were of crimson silk with rows
Of bells and pomegranates and furbelows,
　　Their turbans like blossoming almond-trees.

And so the Three Kings rode into the West,
　　Through the dusk of night, over hill and dell.
And sometimes they nodded with beard on breast,
And sometimes talked, as they paused to rest,
　　With the people they met at some wayside well.

"Of the Child that is born," said Baltasar,
　　"Good people, I pray you, tell us the news;
For we in the East have seen his Star,
And have ridden fast, and have ridden far,
　　To find and worship the King of the Jews."

And the people answered, "You ask in vain;
　　We know of no King but Herod the Great!"
They thought the Wise Men were men insane,
As they spurred their horses across the plain,
　　Like riders in haste, and who cannot wait.

And when they came to Jerusalem,
  Herod the Great, who had heard this thing,
Sent for the Wise Men and questioned them;
And said, "Go down unto Bethlehem,
  And bring me tidings of this new King."

So they rode away; and the Star stood still,
  The only one in the grey of morn;
Yes, it stopped — it stood still of its own free will,
Right over Bethlehem on the hill,
  The City of David, where Christ was born.

And the Three Kings rode through the gate and
        the guard,
  Through the silent street, till their horses
        turned
And neighed as they entered the great inn-yard;
But the windows were closed and the doors were
        barred,
  And only a light in the stable burned.

And cradled there in the scented hay,
  In the air made sweet by the breath of kine,
The little Child in the manger lay,
The Child, that would be King one day
  Of a Kingdom not human but divine.

His mother Mary of Nazareth
  Sat watching beside his place of rest,

Watching the even flow of his breath,
For the joy of life and the terror of death
  Were mingled together in her breast.

They laid their offerings at his feet:
  The gold was their tribute to a King,
The frankincense, with its odour sweet,
Was for the Priest, the Paraclete,
  The myrrh for the body's burying.

And the mother wondered and bowed her head,
  And sat as still as a statue of stone;
Her heart was troubled yet comforted,
Remembering what the Angel had said
  Of an endless reign and of David's throne.

Then the Kings rode out of the city gate,
  With a clatter of hoofs in proud array;
But they went not back to Herod the Great,
For they knew his malice and feared his hate,
  And returned to their homes by another way.

Henry Wadsworth Longfellow

APPENDIX

SUGGESTIONS

FOR TEACHERS AND LEADERS OF
POETRY HOURS

*Primitive ballads have a straightforward felicity; many of them a con-
juring melody as befits verse and music born together. Their gold is
virgin, from the rock strata, and none the better for refining and bur-
nishing. No language is richer in them than the English.*

EDMUND CLARENCE STEDMAN

*The old song of Chevy-Chase is the favourite ballad of the Common People
of England; and Ben Jonson used to say, he had rather have been the
author of it than of all his works. . . . For my own part, I am so pro-
fessed an admirer of this antiquated song, that I shall give my reader a
critic upon it.*

JOSEPH ADDISON

BALLADS are living organisms.[1] If a teacher requires
a pupil to analyze minutely a ballad according to rules
of prosody and literary criticism, the analysis ruth-
lessly destroys its spontaneous folk-spirit. To dissect
a ballad is literary slaughter.

We all know how the cold-blooded analysis of choice
masterpieces destroys forever a pupil's pleasure in
reading them. The teacher of ballad-literature should
use the opposite method to that of literary criticism.
She should make her pupil delight in a ballad for
its own sake; for its unity, its swinging rhythm, its
unself-conscious expressions of emotion, and for the
human life within it.

A ballad treated in this sympathetic manner will
become a thrilling memory for the pupil to carry
through the years. A ballad presented thus has edu-

[1] See Foreword, page vii.

cational values besides that of giving joy. It may be
used to develop the pupil's sense of time and rhythm;
to enlarge his vocabulary; to teach him to express his
thoughts without affectation; to give him ease in sight-
reading of Scottish dialect and old English spelling and
to accustom him to obsolete words. As a memory
exercise for the pupil, the learning and recitation of
ballads is unrivaled; because young people memorize
them without effort. And furthermore, ballads have
dramatic qualities that hold and move a mixed audience of boys and girls of all ages — and of grown folk,
too, for that matter.

But perhaps the most important educational func-
tion of ballad-literature is that of being a safety-valve
for the escape of new, fast-rising feelings and enthu-
siasms of growing boys and girls, feelings that throng
and press for utterance. Young people do not know
how to put them into their own words, but find a
wholesome and satisfying means of expressing their
emotions through learning and reciting ballads or by
reading them aloud.

THE BALLADS IN THIS BOOK

THERE are many versions of old ballads, of some as
many as twenty or more; those most suitable for young
people are given here.

There are included here ballads in Scottish dialect,
and in old English wording with obsolete spelling and
capitalization. These versions may be used with con-
fidence by the teacher, because no pains have been
spared in collating them by authoritative texts.[1]

[1] See Acknowledgments, p. xv, and Foreword, p. vii.

Even such differing forms as *o'* or *o; wi'* or *wi; e'e* or *ee; then* for *than* or *than* for *then;* and variations of proper names, as in "Proud Lady Margaret," have been followed according to the text used.

Quotation marks, only, have been added for the convenience of the young folk. A few objectionable, but unimportant, words have been changed. In the version of "Chevy-Chase," Bishop Percy's *Folio Manuscript* has been followed with a few emendations from his *Reliques*, including the capitalization of the first letter of each line. The *Folio Manuscript* is more authoritative than the *Reliques*.

Some of the ballads and verses which follow the old forms given by collectors are: "The Stormy Winds Do Blow," p. 2; "Sir Patrick Spens," p. 3; "The Dæmon Lover," p. 7; "Chevy-Chase," p. 21; "Proud Lady Margaret," p. 62; "The Famous Flower of Serving-Men," p. 65; "The Young Tamlane," p. 255; "Thomas the Rhymer," p. 93; "The Wee Wee Man," p. 114; "The Earl of Mar's Daughter," p. 115; "Kemp Owyne," p. 122; "Fair Anny of Roch-royal," p. 191; "The Cruel Sister," p. 196; "Blancheflour and Jelly-florice," p. 209; "The Gay Goss-Hawk," p. 218; "Bonny Baby Livingston," p. 224; "Young Beichan and Susie Pye," p. 237; "The Wife of Usher's Well," p. 263; "Sir Roland," p. 265; the Robin Hood ballads, p. 290 ff.; "True Valour," p. 355; "Pilgrimage," p. 351; "Peace," p. 356.

In striking and pleasing contrast to the old ballads are the modern ones with capitalization to please modern children. It may be noted that the texts of Keats's "La Belle Dame," and Campbell's "Earl March," are different from the versions usually included in children's ballad-books. The texts followed here are those most lately approved by literary critics.

PROGRAMME

FOR A YEAR OF BALLAD-READING AND STUDY

ONE PERIOD A WEEK FOR FORTY WEEKS

WAYS in which ballads may be used in the classroom or during Poetry Hours:

1. *Reading aloud for development of literary taste.* This is the most important educational use of ballads. The teacher should read them aloud to the class, giving them all their native swing and quick pulsation. The minstrels, who composed them, often accented words to suit the length of their lines; so if the reader will lend her voice to the rhythm of the verse, the accents will fall where they belong. Such words as *country, harper, singer, damsel, lady,* and *battle* should sometimes be accented on the last syllable, as *countrý, singér, harpér, ladý.*

2. *Memorizing and reciting.* Boys and girls enjoy learning ballads by heart. They do so with astonishing ease. The teacher may assign one ballad to the whole class; or she may divide the class into sections and assign a ballad to each section. This should be done at least two or three weeks before the period for recitation. The teacher may then call on one or more of the pupils to recite.

3. *Story-telling from the ballads.* The teacher may read aloud a ballad. She should read it two or three times to the class. Then the pupils may retell it in story form either orally or in writing.

4. *Dramatization.* Ballads are so dramatic and simple in their movement that they may be easily acted in the schoolroom with or without improvised scenery and costumes. The teacher or pupil may read aloud the ballad, while some of the boys and girls act it out in dumb show; or, better yet, the actors may recite the lines that belong to their parts, and the teacher may read aloud the descriptive parts only. Whenever a refrain occurs, as in "The Stormy Winds Do Blow," the whole class may join in reciting it.

5. *Writing from memory.* The teacher may assign a ballad to the class to learn by heart; and then she may have the class write it out from memory following closely the spelling, punctuation, and dialect of the text.

6. *Original ballad-writing.* Young people are natural ballad-makers. At the end of the year, after memorizing and reciting ballads and listening to them read aloud, the pupils will be so saturated with ballad-spirit and meter, that ballad-writing will be a second nature. The teacher may then tell, very briefly but interestingly, the plot of a ballad, and let the pupils put it into original verses, giving them a week or two in which to do so. After this exercise the teacher may assign a local legend or story for practice in original ballad-writing.

The Programme that is given here is merely suggestive. All the ballads in the book are good to read aloud, and most of them may be dramatized or memorized. The course presented below shows a teacher how she may, by progressive steps, develop her pupils' taste for ballad-literature, and prepare them to appreciate more mature forms of narrative poetry, such as metrical romances and epics.

COURSE FOR FORTY WEEKS — ONE PERIOD A
WEEK

1st Week. Reading aloud: The Laidley Worm O' Spindleston-Heughs, p. 148.

2d Week. Reading aloud: Little Billee, p. 159; Brian O'Linn,
p. 160; Dicky of Ballyman, p. 162; The Cinder King,
p. 167.

3d Week. Dramatization: The Stormy Winds Do Blow,
p. 2; The Noble Riddle, p. 208; "Earl March looked
on his dying child," p. 203.

4th Week. Reading aloud: The Lady of Shalott, p. 124; The
Singing Leaves, p. 131.

5th Week. Dramatization: Kemp Owyne, p. 122; The Erl-
King, p. 86.

6th Week. Reading aloud: Robin Hood and Little John,
p. 291; Robin Hood and Clorinda, p. 297.

7th Week. Dramatization: Ballad of the Oysterman, p. 164;
Earl Haldan's Daughter, p. 58; The Greeting of Kynast,
p. 74; A Tragic Story, p. 158.

8th Week. Reading aloud (Halloween Week): The Spell,
p. 254; Sir Roland, p. 265; The Cruel Sister, p. 196;
The Skeleton in Armour, p. 270.

9th Week. Dramatization: Glenara, p. 212; The Dæmon
Lover, p. 7.

10th Week. Reading aloud: King Alfred and the Shepherd,
p. 176.

11th Week. Story-telling from the Ballads: Young Beichan
and Susie Pye, p. 237.

12th Week. Reading aloud: The Fairy Thorn, p. 87; The
Kelpie of Corrievreckan, p. 97.

13th Week. Memorizing and reciting: True Valour, p. 355;
The Touchstone, p. 347; Barclay of Ury, p. 341; Pilgrimage, p. 351.

14th Week. Reading aloud: The Heart of the Bruce, p. 333.

15th Week. Memorizing and reciting (for Christmas): The
Royal Court, p. 353; Peace, p. 356; The Three Kings,
p. 357.

16th Week. Reading aloud: Lady Clare, p. 59; Sir Galahad,
p. 348.

17th Week. Story-telling from the Ballads: The Earl of Mar's Daughter, p. 115.

18th Week. Reading aloud: Ballad of Meikle-Mouthed Meg, p. 32.

19th Week. Dramatization: The Gay Goss-Hawk, p. 218; Thomas the Rhymer, p. 93.

20th Week. Reading aloud: Young Tamlane, p. 255.

21st Week. Memorizing and reciting: Lord Lovel, p. 204; The Beggar-Maid, p. 214; The Sands of Dee, p. 190; Lochinvar, p. 215.

22d Week. Reading aloud: Fair Anny of Roch-royal, p. 191; Bonny Baby Livingston, p. 224.

23d Week. Story-telling from the Ballads: Blancheflour and Jellyflorice, p. 209.

24th Week. Reading aloud: The Child of Elle, p. 244.

25th Week. Writing from memory: The Birth o' Robin Hood, p. 290; The Wee Wee Man, p. 114.

26th Week. Reading aloud: More Modern Ballad of Chevy-Chase, p. 21.

27th Week. Story-telling from the Ballads: Cochrane's Bonny Grizzy, p. 70; The Frolicksome Duke, p. 169.

28th Week. Reading aloud: May of the Moril Glen, p. 138.

29th Week. Writing from memory: The Wife of Usher's Well, p. 263.

30th Week. Reading aloud: Sir Patrick Spens, p. 3; Hynd Horn, p. 231.

31st Week. Writing from memory: Proud Lady Margaret, p. 62.

32d Week. Reading aloud: Song of the Outlaw Murray, p. 301.

33d Week. Original ballad-writing: Barbara Allen's Cruelty, p. 201; Alice Brand, p. 81; The Famous Flower of Serving-Men, p. 65.

34th Week. Reading aloud: The Eve of St. John, p. 279.

35th Week. Memorizing and reciting: The Fairy Tempter, p. 80; The Luck of Edenhall, p. 135; La Belle Dame sans Merci, p. 9.

36th Week. Reading aloud: The Mermaid, p. 10.

37th Week. Original ballad-writing: King James the First and the Tinkler, p. 173; Valentine and Ursine, p. 314; Belted Will, p. 47.

38th Week. Reading aloud: Kilmeny, p. 101.

39th Week. Original ballad-writing: The teacher may assign a subject for this — a local legend or story of a patriotic or historical event.

40th Week. Entertainment for Parents and Friends of Pupils: The ballad-course may close with an afternoon or evening entertainment. This may be made delightful. All the pupils should take part in the exercises.

Many of the old ballads are set to charming ancient tunes, and may be sung by the whole school. Banjo or guitar accompaniment is specially appropriate to ballad airs. Musical scores for some of the ballads in this book — "The Cruel Sister" ("The Twa Sisters"), "Hynd Horn," "Sir Patrick Spens," "Young Beichan," "Proud Lady Margaret," "The Famous Flower of Serving-Men," and "Lord Lovel" — may be found in Professor Child's *English and Scottish Popular Ballads*, large edition, part 10. If the music of old ballads is not obtainable, then popular, well-known ballads, such as "Annie Laurie," "Ben Bolt," and "Loch Lomond," may be sung in their stead.

The following outline for an entertainment may be varied to suit the abilities and interests of the boys and girls who are to take part:

PROGRAMME FOR AN ENTERTAINMENT

One or more ballads sung by the pupils.
Recitation.
Dramatization.
Ballad-reading.
A ballad solo.
Recitation.

Reading of the best original ballad composed by a pupil.
Dramatization.
Recitation.
Close: the audience and pupils may sing one or more
    popular, well-known American ballads, such as may
    be found in any good song-collection.

In making up her Programme, the teacher should
avoid selecting very long ballads for memorization and
recitation. It is best to let the pupils who are to recite,
choose the ballads they like best. She should be care-
ful to balance her Programme with verses of all kinds
— grave and gay, sad and weird, romantic and historical. She should so artistically compose her Programme
that it will play on the emotions of her audience, moving it from laughter to tears, from awe to the heroic.
That is what ballads are for, to touch the heart, as
well as the head.

FOR LIBRARIANS AND SOCIAL WORKERS

THIS entire course, as outlined for forty weeks, may
be followed by Librarians and Social Workers. They
may, however, shorten the Programme or alter it to
suit the occasion.

GLOSSARY AND INDEXES

GLOSSARY

A', all
Aboon, above
Abune, above
Acton, stuffed leather jacket worn under coat-of-mail
Ae, one, single, sole, mere
Aff, off, oft
Aften, often
Aiblins, perhaps
Aik, oak
Ain, own
Airn, iron
Alake, alas!
Alane, alone
Amang, among
An, and
Ance, once
Ane, one
Ankers, anchors
Anse, once
Ask, newt, lizard
Atabal, Moorish kettledrum
Attour, above
Auld, old
Awa' *or* **awa**, away
Awn, own
Ayme, aim

Bairn *or* **bairnie**, child
Baith, both
Bale, fire, faggot
Ban, band
Bane, bone
Bartizan, a small overhanging turret jutting out from the top of a tower
Bash, beat, smash in

Beacon, a fire lighted on a height as a danger signal to call together warriors to repel the enemy
Bedeen, immediately, forthwith; often used as an expletive, or as a rhyme-word at the end of a line
Belay, lie in the way for
Beltan *or* **Beltane**, a Celtic pagan festival celebrated on May Day or May 3d, by lighting bonfires on hilltops
Bent, coarse grass, open field, sandy knoll covered with coarse grass, the hollow of a hill
Berserk, ancient Norse warrior who raged with fury in battle
Bigged, built
Bigly, pleasant to live in, spacious
Bill'e, comrade, brother
Birk, birch
Birkie, lively
Birling, drinking
Bla, blow
Black Rood Stone, The Black Rood of Melrose, a crucifix of supposedly great sanctity
Blee, colour, complexion
Blew, blue
Blin, cease, stop
Blude, blood
Borrow, set free, deliver, ransom
Boud, behoved, was obliged
Bouir, bower
Boun', bound, bound home

Bour, bower

Bout, bolt

Bower or bowir, lady's chamber, a house, a rustic cottage

Bra', fine, handsome, brave

Brae, down, a slope of a hill

Braid, broad. "A braid letter"; a letter on a broad sheet, or a long letter

Brak, broke

Brake, thicket, a place overgrown with ferns, shrubs, and brambles

Brash, sickness

Brast, burst

Brattle, race, hurry

Braw, comely, handsome, well-dressed

Bree, brows, eyebrows

Brode, breed

Broom, the Genista, a shrub with bright golden flowers

Bughts, pens

Burd alone, by himself, solitary

Burn, brook

Busked, dressed, adorned

But and, and also

Bygane, gone by

Byre, cow-house

Cade lamb, lamb brought up by hand, pet lamb

Callant, lad

Cam' or cam, came

Capapie, cap-à-pié, from head to foot. Armed cap-à-pié, armed from head to foot

Carl or carle, churl

Carline, old woman, peasant woman

Carlish, churlish, uncivilized

Carp, tell tales, sing or chant ballads

Castle-yate, castle-gate

Caul or cauld, cold

Channerin', fretting

Chaps, jaw, chops

Cheik, cheek

Child or childe, a youth of gentle birth

Christentie, Christendom

Claith, cloth

Claymore, large sword

Cleedin, clothing

Clour, bump on the head from a heavy blow

Clouted, heavy and patched

Clouted cream, clotted cream

Cloutie, patched, ragged

Coft, bought

Cold, could

Contrair, contrary, opposed

Corbie, raven

Cosh, quiet

Coud, could

Couldna, could not

Couthy, friendly, kind, loving

Cow-me-doo, Coo-my-dove, loving name for a dove

Craig, neck, throat

Craw, crow

Crawed, crowed

Cum, come, came

Cumbruk, cambric

Cushat, ring-dove, wood-pigeon

Dae, doe

Dantonit, daunted

Daunton, daunt, subdue

Daw, dawn

Dean or den, dell, narrow glen

Death-thraw, death-struggle

Dee, do, die

Degree, rank. "Served him in his own degree," offered him respect according to his rank

Deil, Devil
Dinna, do not
Dochter, daughter
Doo, dove
Dought, should be able to, can
Doun, down
Dour *or* **doure,** hard, severe, savage
Dove, word of endearment for one pure and gentle
Downa, cannot
Drap, drop
Drapp'd, dropped
Dree, be able, stand. "As fast as he might dree," as fast as he could, undergo, suffer
Drumlie, gloomy
Duddis, poor clothes, tatters, duds
Dule, grief
Dun, dark coloured, of a dull brown colour
Dune, done

Eccho, echo
Eche, each
E'e *or* **ee,** eye
Effeir, pomp, circumstance, bearing, garb, panoply
Eident, unrestingly
Eildon, a high hill with three-pointed summit, overlooking Melrose town. Eildon Tree, the spot where Thomas the Rhymer is supposed to have uttered his prophecies
Eiry, eery, weird, dreary, gloomy, fear-inspiring
Eldern, old
Elritch, elvish
Elyed, vanished
Eneuch, enough
Enoo, enough

Ere, ever
Erle, earl
Erlish, elvish
Erst, first, formerly
Even cloth, smooth cloth, with nap well shorn
Eve of St. John, Midsummer Day, June 24
Eyne, eyes

Fa' *or* **fa,** fall, befall
Faem *or* **faeme,** foam
Fairing, gift, present given at a fair
Fallow deer, small European deer, of a fallow, or pale yellow colour
Fand, found
Fa'se, false
Fashes, troubles
Faulds, folds
Faured, favoured
Fause, false
Feckless, weak, feeble, silly
Fee, wealth
Feircly, fiercely
Fell, sharply, severely, keen, eager
Fere, mate, consort, companion
Ferlie, marvel, wonder
Fidge, fidget
Flang, flung about, skipped
Flatter, float
Flee, flay
Flude, flood
Forbode, "Over God's forbode"; God forbid!
Forfaulted, forfeited
Forgather, meet
Forhooyed, forsook
Fornenst, opposite to
Fou, full
Frae, from
Freit, a good or bad omen

Frith, wood, enclosed land

Fu' or **fu,** very, full, very much, fully

Gad, bar

Gae, go

Galliard, an old-time brisk dance

Gane, suffice, gone

Gang, go

Gar, make, cause, do

Garr'd, made, caused

Gear, possessions, property, cattle

Geck, mock

Gerfalcon, large falcon of the Northlands

Gi'd, went

Gie, give

Gien, given

Gif, if

Gillore, gallore, in plenty

Gimp, jimp, slender

Gin, if, suppose, granted it be so, whether

Glaive, sword

Gleg, spry, quick

Gleid, spark

Gloamin, twilight

Good b'w' ye, good be with ye, good-bye, derived from the phrase "God be with you," or "with ye"

Gos-hawk or **goss-hawk,** large hawk

Goud, gold

Gouden, golden

Goun, gown

Goups, handfuls

Goved, stared

Gowan, daisy

Gowd, gold

Gowdn, golden

Graith, make ready

Grange, farmhouse with outer buildings

Gratte, wept, cried

Greet, weep

Grew hound, greyhound, grey

Grewis, greyhounds

Groat, old English silver coin worth fourpence issued from 1351–1662

Gude, good

Gudely, goodly

Guid, good

Guise, manner, behaviour

Gurly, grim, growling, surly

Gyant, giant

Ha' or **ha,** hall

Had, hold

Hadna or **hadnae,** had not

Hae, have

Haggis, Scotch dish made of a sheep's maw filled with minced meat, onions, and other ingredients mixed and cooked with oatmeal

Hail, whole

Half-fou, two pecks, half a bushel

Haly, holy

Hame, home

Han, hand

Hap, chance, fortune

Happed, covered, wrapped

Haud, hold, keep

Hauld, hold

Hay, "Went forth to view the hay," went to see how the hay was coming on

Heely, slowly, gently

Her lane, by herself

Heugh, steep hill, glen with overhanging sides

Hie, haste, high

Hindberrye, wild raspberry

Hing, hang

Hingers, hangers

Hinny *or* hinnie, honey

His lane, by himself

Holland *or* hollin, coarse linen, unbleached or dyed brown

Holt, piece of woodland, a woody hill

Holy Grail, the holy cup, used by the Lord Christ at the Last Supper, was called in medieval romances, "The Holy Grail"

Houf, haunt

Hoysed, hoisted

Hurden, coarse linen or hempen fabric

Hye *or* hie, haste

Hynd, Hynde, *or* Hind, young, courteous, gracious, gentle

Hypp, fruit of the dog-rose

I' *or* i, in

Ilk *or* ilka, every, each

Intill, into, in

Its lane, by itself

Jaw, wave

Jawes, surges

Jet, strut

Jimp, slender, slim

Jimply, barely, scarcely, hardly, narrowly

Joup, petticoat

Kaim, comb

Kaimin, combing

Kane, tribute

Kell, a cap of network for a woman's hair

Kemb, comb

Kemed, combed

Ken, know

Kendna, did not know

Kenned *or* kend, knew

Kep, catch, stop

Keppit, caught

Kirk, church

Kittle, difficult to manage, risky, ticklish

Knaw, know

Kynast, castle in Northern Germany

Kythe, appear

Laddie, diminutive of lad

Laidley, loathly, loathsome

Laird, squire, lord of the manor, owner of lands

Laith, loath

Lan, land

Lane, lone

Lanely, lonely

Lang, long

Lap, sprang, leaped

Lappered, clotted

Lat, let

Laverock, lark

Lax, relief

Lease, lease (of bucks), three bucks

Leme, gleam

Lend, grant, give

Lettn, let

Leven, lawn, glade, open ground in the forest

Leveret, hare

Liffe, life

Lift, air, sky

Liften, lifted

Lighters, horse-blinders or blinkers

Liken, make like

Lish, lithe, supple, agile

Lither, lazy, idle, worthless, wicked

Littand, staining, defiling

Live-lang, live-long

Lo'ed, loved

Lood, loved

Loof, palm of the hand

Loon, fellow, rogue

Loot, let, allowed

Lout, bend, bow, lean

Lowed, glowed

Lown, calm, serene, silent, quiet

Lug, ear

Luve, love

Lyart, grey, hoary

Lydder, lazy, idle, loathsome

Lyon's moods, this possibly means like the mood or pluck of lions; authorities differ as to readings

Lyth, member, joint

Mae, more

Maik *or* **maike,** mate

Mair, more

Make, mate, consort

March *or* **Marches,** border-frontier, the boundary between England and Scotland. Warden of the March, governor of the Scotch Border

Marrow, mate, wife, husband

Martinmas, mass or feast of St. Martin, November 11

Maun, must

Maunna, must not

Mavis, thrush

May, maid

Meet, scant, close

Meikle, much, great

Merl *or* **merle,** blackbird

Merk *or* **mark,** about 13s. 4d. in the English money of the time

Mess, mass

Mickle, much, great

Middle, waist

Midsummer Day, June 24

Minny *or* **minnie,** mother

Mirk, dark

Mither, mother

Monmouth Cap, flat round cap formerly worn by English soldiers and sailors. Shakespeare mentions it in *Henry V*

Mony *or* **monie,** many, money

Mote, may

Mountain-mere, mountain-lake

Muir, moor

Na, no, not

Nae, no

Naething, nothing

Nane, none

Nappy, heady, strong

Neer, never, ne'er

Neest, nearest, next

Neir, never, ne'er

Neist, next

Nicht, night

Nowt, neat cattle

Nurice *or* **nourice,** nurse

O' *or* **o,** of

O'erword, refrain, call, cry

Ony, any

Ower, over

Owre, before, over

Palfray, small saddle-horse for ladies, palfrey

Pall, cloak, mantle

Palmer, Pilgrim returned from Holy Land bearing, as a badge, a branch of palm

Paughty, haughty

Philabeg, highland kilt

Pibroch, a Highland dirge or martial air, a kind of wild, irregular music, performed on the bagpipe

Pickle, choice

Pin, an implement for raising the latch of a door, *see* tirled

Pine, suffering, pain

Plait, fold, plate

Plate-jack, coat-armour

Pock-puddings, bag-puddings

Prie, attain

Prieven, attained

Prin, pin

Pu' *or* **pu,** pull

Pu'd, pulled

Putten, put

Quarry, slaughtered game

Quean, saucy girl or young woman

Rad, afraid

Rade, rode

Rae, roe

Raike, range

Rail, woman's jacket

Ravin, violent

Raw, row

Ray, array

Reavers, robbers

Reaving, thieving, robbing

Rede, counsel

Reek, smoke

Reifed, stolen, plundered

Reifery, robbery, plundering

Rife, abounding

Rins, runs

Rock, distaff used in spinning

Rode *or* **Rood,** Holy Cross, crucifix, *see also* Black Rood of Melrose

Roul, roll

Roun' *or* **roun,** round, around about

Rowan Tree, mountain ash, which is also called the Fairies' tree because Witches and Evil Spirits are said to fear it

Rowed, rolled, wound

Rowt, roar

St. John's Eve, Midsummer Day, June 24

Sae, so

Saft, soft, softly

Saikless, innocent

Sained, crossed, blessed, hallowed

Sair, sore, painful, very much

Sall, shall

Satten, satin

Saul, soul

Saut, salt

Sax, six

Scallop-shell, a small fluted shell. In the middle ages, Pilgrims used to wear scallop-shells as badges of their pilgrimage

Scaur, steep bank overhanging a river, a cliff

Scorke, struck

Scot-free, the word " scot " means payment, fine, reckoning, tax. Scot-free means free from payment; also, without harm, unhurt, safe

Screen, plaid, cloak, large scarf thrown over the head

Scrip, small bag, Pilgrim's pouch

Sea-maw, gull, sea mew

Sen, sent

Sets with, suits

Seymar, loose robe

Share of Truth, ploughshare of Truth — used as figurative language

Shathmont, measure from top of extended thumb to the extremity of palm — six inches

Shaw, thicket, copse

Sheave, slice

Sheen, bright, shining

Sheugh, trench, ditch, furrow

Shoon, shoes

Shot-window, projecting window in the staircase of old Scotch wooden house

Sic, such

Sichin, sighing

Sicken, such

Siller, silver

Simmer, summer

Sin, since

Sin, " Thankless sins the gifts he gets," probably means to hold them in slight esteem. (Footnote in Scott)

Skaith, harm, an injury

Skald, ancient Scandinavian poet or bard

Skaw, promontory or low cape

Skeely, skilful

Skelping, moving rapidly

Skoal, hail!

Sleeks, makes smooth

Slogan, war-cry of the Scottish Highlanders

Sma or sma', small

Snaw, snow

Snell, sharp, keen, shrill, bitter

Snickersnee, sailor's sheath-knife or bowie knife

Snood, hair-band

Snoove, go smoothly and constantly

Solan, gannet, solan-goose

Solempne, solemn

Sommer, summer

Sonsy or Sonsie, plump

Sorning, spunging, obtruding

Soudron or Southron, southern, the English

Spak, spake, spoke

Spankie, sprightly, friskly, smart

Speer, ask

Sperthe, battle-axe

Spier, spear

Sta, stole

Stane, stone

Stead, dwelling-place

Steek, stitch

Step minnie, stepmother

Stern-light, starlight

Stour or stoure, dust, skirmish, struggle, battle

Stown, stolen

Strack, struck

Stran, strand

Strang, strong

Strath, valley thro' which a river runs

Stron, the end of a ridge of hills

Stude, stood

Sucket, sugar-plum

Suld, should

Sune, soon

Swa'd, swelled

Syke, marsh

Syle, soil

Syne, then, afterward, since

Tae, toe

Ta'en or taen, taken

Taffetie, taffeta

Taiglit, tarried

Taiken, token

Tak, take

Tald, told

Tale, number, count

Tane, taken

Tauld, told

Teind, tithe

Tent, take care of, watch, guard

Tent, Spanish wine of a deep red colour

Termagant, a pagan deity, whom the Crusaders said was worshipped by the Mohammedans

Tett, lock of hair or of a mane

Thae, these, those

Then, than

Thie, thigh

Thimber, heavy, massive

Thir, those, these

Thysell, thyself

Till, to

Tinkler, tinker

Tint, lost

Tirled or **tirld,** twist or rattle. "Tirld at the pin," see Pin

Tod, fox

Toom, empty

Touchstone, a kind of compact stone used to test gold and silver

Toun, hamlet, farmhouse

Trailed, dragged

Tree, wood, made of wood

Trow, trust, believe, think

Tryst, appointed place of meeting, also appointment to meet

Turtle-doo, turtle-dove

Twa, two

Twae, two

Twin'd, deprived, parted

Ugsome, exciting disgust, abhorrent

Ummeled, unmixed, pure

Upgive, avow, own up

Upo, on, to, with, at, in

Vair, squirrel-fur

Vaunt-brace, armour for the body

Verra, very

Wa' or **wa,** wall

Wad, would

Wae, woe

Waik, glade

Wained, carried, removed

Waith, wandering, roaming, straying

Wall-wightmen, picked, strong men

Waly, exclamation of admiration

Wan, won

Wap, wrap, stuff

War'd, expended, used

Warden, keeper, guardian. Warden of the March, governor of the Scotch Border

Warden Pies, pies made of warden pears — large pears

Warld, world

Warlock, sorcerer, wizard

Warse, worse

Warst, worst

Wasna, was not

Wassail-bout, drinking revel, carouse

Wat, wet

Wauking, watch, walk

Weel, well

Weet, wet

Weir, to collect and drive cattle

We'rd, Destiny, Fate, Fortune

Well-kent, well-known

Wene, recess

Wer-wolf, person transformed into a wolf

Westlin, Western

Wha, who

Whare, where

Whaten, what sort, what kind

Whidderan, whizzing

Whin-bushes, furze, gorse

Wi' or **wi,** with

Win, wind

Win in, get in

Winna, will not

Wis, know

Withouten *or* withoutten, without

Wodensday, Wednesday, derived from the name of the Anglo-Saxon god, Woden; which name meant " the furious " or " the mighty warrior "

Wold, would

Wold, open tract of country

Woned, dwelt

Wot, know

Wud, would

Y *or* I, a prefix to many Middle English words, often used (specially with past-participles) to intensify their meanings

Yallow, yellow

Yate, gate

Y-built, *see above* Y or I

Yer sel, yourself

Yett, gate

Yont, beyond

Yorlin, yellow-hammer

Yoursell, yourself

Yowlit, yowled, howled, yelped

Y-wis, i-wis, certainly, surely, truly, to wit, indeed

Y-wrought, *see above* Y or I

SUBJECT INDEX

INDEX OF FIRST LINES

INDEX OF TITLES AND AUTHORS

With references from titles of other ballad-versions

WITHDRAWN

JUL 0 3 2024

DAVID O. McKAY LIBRARY
BYU-IDAHO